Praise for *A Jew Grows In Brooklyn*

"Jake Ehrenreich is a funny and articulate storyteller. This is a magically, well-written universal story of identity and tradition that anyone, Jew or Gentile, can relate to. *A Jew Grows in Brooklyn* is so deeply rooted with honesty, humor, and emotion in every turn of the page, you will soon find it growing in your heart."

—**Neil Sedaka**, singer and songwriter

"As another Jew who grew in Brooklyn and punched a 'spaldeen' two sewers, I laughed out loud and cried tears of nostalgia at Ehrenreich's stories. Even people who grew up elsewhere will enjoy. So go ahead, why not?—read it and kvell."

—**Alan Dershowitz**, bestselling author
and Harvard law professor

"I loved reading *A Jew Grows in Brooklyn*. Jake Ehrenreich has written a joyous reflection on his life that anyone can relate to. It made me think of my own childhood and I recalled my parents in a most loving and positive light. The spirit of this book reminds me of an adage I often heard growing up in New York, 'When you're in love, the whole world is Jewish.' And I'm a goy!"

—**Ken Howard**, Emmy Award–winning actor
and president of the Screen Actors Guild (SAG)

"Mr. Ehrenreich has more than a sense of humor, he has a sense of humanity that dives into the common river of human experience and gives voice to the silent, and sometimes forgotten, depths of our own precious memories. He is a storyteller-philosopher par excellence well worth the read."

—actress **Tovah Feldshuh**, six-time
Tony and Emmy nominee

D0169836

"Despite a childhood shadowed by the Holocaust and family illness, Jake Ehrenreich has an ebullience and a humor that makes his memoir sheer pleasure. From Brooklyn to the Catskills to the Village . . . he remembers it all and tells it with a tender, funny, and thoughtful voice."

—**Joan Micklin Silver**, Director of
Hester Street, Crossing Delancey

"You don't have to be Jewish to love Jake's wry take on childhood, family, tragedy, the Beatles, and Alka Seltzer. Reading Jake Ehrenreich is like eating a pastrami sandwich while playing stickball: wild, crazy, fun—and you may find yourself choking up."

—**Lenore Skenazy**, author of *Free-Range Kids: Giving Our Children the Freedom We Had Without Going Nuts with Worry*

"Jake Ehrenreich has written an uplifting memoir that doubles as an inspiring user-friendly primer on how to be comfortable in your own skin. But instead of sitting in a classroom or therapist's office, Ehrenreich's tone makes you feel like you're shooting the breeze in your best friend's living room. A Jew may be growing in Brooklyn, but a marvelous, compassionate storyteller is also growing before our eyes. Ehrenreich hits the mark with his honest and inspiring quest for identity and redemption."

—**Scott Benarde**, author of
Stars of David: Rock 'n' Roll's Jewish Stories

"Jake Ehrenreich, a hip guy who made it—but deep down, just a kid from Brooklyn. The son of Holocaust survivors, Jake takes you on a fascinating personal journey as he tells his story with warmth, depth, fun, and love. He almost makes you feel like part of his extended family while he helps to remind us that who we are has a lot to do with our past. This is a great, funny, and inspiring book—full of personal insight."

—**Pat Phillips**, Producer, Carnegie Hall, Songwriters Hall of Fame, Board Member Grammy Awards

Praise for the Stage Show

"Beautiful . . . touching . . . funny . . . 'A Jew Grows in Brooklyn' has a lot in common with [Billy Crystal's] '700 Sundays' . . . you don't have to be Jewish or Brooklynish . . . dazzling!"

—*The New York Times*

"Anybody with concern for the family should run to see this show. Very entertaining and thought provoking. I loved this show!"

—**Dr. Ruth Westheimer**

"Aims straight for your heart . . . Beautiful . . . a Knockout . . . somewhere two loving parents are *kvelling* over the son who did them proud!"

—*The Miami Herald*

"Ehrenreich is a wonderful storyteller. It also helps that his first-generation immigrant story about his Holocaust survivor parents and his desire to be an 'all-American regular inner-city kid' is engaging, poignant and, at times, hilarious. Ehrenreich's loving tribute to his family is a winner!"

—*The Palm Beach Post*

"Has a warm glow all its own!"

—*The Chicago Tribune*

"Endearing and nostalgic . . . What's not to love?"

—*The Philadelphia Inquirer*

"Cheerful, funny, and charming! Displaying wry, self deprecating humor, and a profound appreciation of his heritage, Ehrenreich cajoles and charms through a boomer coming of age tale, skipping backward to his family's tribulations in the old country and forward to his rock & roll adventures and fatherhood."

—*Time Out New York*

"Ehrenreich's delicious, nostalgic, poignant, and, at time times, hilarious two hour marathon autobiographical retrospective of growing up in Brooklyn is pure joy! He had the audience roaring!"

—The Forward

"Overwhelming and beautiful. It took a few days for my feet to touch the ground again after this production and performance. Inspiring stories of love, happiness and renewed life on the highest level. I consider this the most cherished and long lasting gift—talent, courage, and inspiration to bring laughter to every dark corner of this world."

—Avi Mizrachi, Executive Director,
Foundation for Holocaust Education Projects

"Join in the homecoming. Ehrenreich would win over a symposium of Episcopal ministers from Boston!"

—The Sun Sentinel

"It's a ball! Show stopping!"

—New York Daily News

"Through sometimes poignant, sometimes hilarious stories about his family, Ehrenreich weaves together haimish wisdom and a modern sensibility."

—New York Magazine

"Both funny and heartbreaking. Ehrenreich's production is a touching tribute to his parents, Holocaust survivors, and the travails of a first-generation kid navigating all-American waters. His memories are touching and sad, but also life affirming. Traversing a cross-cultural thicket is a challenge; to make us laugh and cry while he does it is artistry."

—Traveler's USA

"Jake Ehrenreich croons, reminisces, kibitzes, and breathlessly revisits the golden age of entertainment . . . a singing valentine!"

—The New Yorker

"Wonderfully enjoyable!"

—Broadway After Dark

"Speaks to anyone hoping to live out the American Dream."

—**ABC TV**

"Lots of laughs but also very serious. This hit show has taken New York by storm and played to sold-out audiences since it opened. Ehrenreich does it all, and you don't have to be Jewish to appreciate his message."

—**FOX TV**

"A personality that you just can't help but like!"

—*The Village Voice*

"At once funny and sad . . . Ehrenreich shines!"

—*Back Stage*

"Jake Ehrenreich distills a lifetime of experience into *A Jew Grows in Brooklyn*!"

—*Playbill*

"Delightful and hilarious."

—**AOL Online**

"The amount of heart that Ehrenreich possesses is overwhelming—you will fall in love with this guy, his family and his nostalgic affections for Jewish humor and baby boomer Brooklyn culture."

—*amNewYork*

"A delightful journey with all the joy, tenderness, and heartbreak of being a Jew."

—**WOR Radio New York**

"Jake Ehrenreich is supremely gifted . . . he tells his family's story lovingly, honestly and with great humor."

—**PBS TV**

"Joyous, wise and wonderful. Take your synagogue, take your church. Everyone should see this show!"

—**Msgr. Thomas Hartman** and
Rabbi Marc Gellman, TV's *The God Squad*

A JEW GROWS IN BROOKLYN

The Curious Reflections of a First-Generation American

Jake Ehrenreich

Health Communications, Inc.
Deerfield Beach, Florida
www.hcibooks.com

Library of Congress Cataloging-in-Publication Data

Ehrenreich, Jake.
A Jew grows in Brooklyn : the curious reflections of a first generation American /
Jake Ehrenreich.
    p. cm.
    ISBN-13: 978-0-7573-1466-7
    ISBN-10: 0-7573-1466-X
    1. Ehrenreich, Jake.   2. Jews—New York (State)—New York—Biography.
3. Children of Holocaust survivors—New York (State)—New York—Biography.
4. Children of immigrants—New York (State)—New York—Biography.   5. Jewish
dramatists—21st century—Biography.   6. Dramatists, American—21st century—
Biography.   7. Brooklyn (New York, N.Y.)—Biography.   I. Title.
F128.9.J5E44 2010
974.7'04924—dc22
                                  2010003149

Publisher: Health Communications, Inc.
      3201 S.W. 15th Street
      Deerfield Beach, FL 33442–8190

Cover design by Justin Rothkowitz
Interior design by Dawn Von Strolly Grove
Interior formatting by Lawna Patterson Oldfield

For my parents and my sisters,
and the family I never knew.
But most of all for
Lisa and Dovy.

CONTENTS

SETTING THE STAGE

"The greatest thing in this world is not so much
where we are, but in what direction we are moving."

−Oliver Wendell Holmes, Jr.

I ANXIOUSLY WAITED IN THE BACK of the social hall at the community center in Washington Township, New Jersey, and watched the eight (yes, eight) audience members settle in as I prepared to go onstage for the 2005 premiere of my comedy/drama/ musical "Growing Up in America." *My God, What was I doing?!*

I was already in my forties, I had a beautiful wife and son, and I was making a great living as a musician and performer. *Who needs this?* I asked myself, but I already knew the answer. Somehow, I'd always known that I would one day have to tell this story. *I* needed this.

I bounded onto the stage and began singing, playing instruments, and telling the scripted stories of my life as the first-born son of Holocaust survivors, of my Brooklyn childhood and Catskills summers, of caring for my mother and two sisters as they each succumbed to early Alzheimer's disease, of my intensely hardworking father, of finding love, and of how, after a long journey, the story came full circle with the birth of my son, Joseph Dov-Behr Ehrenreich.

1

I got some laughs and tears—and as the week wore on, more than a few audience members. After the first few days, word spread like wildfire. By the end of the week, we were sold out. Eventually, "Growing Up in America" became "A Jew Grows in Brooklyn" and went on to break box-office records at the historic Lambs Theater in the heart of Broadway. We played in New York City for a year and half and have been filling houses across the country ever since.

The look in the eyes of audience members as I see them channel their own childhoods, the stories they share with me after the show, and the special bond we form together is something I may never be able to re-create. But I hope to create something similar with this book. No matter where my life and career take me in the future, I will always return to this honest story of hope and renewal.

In part, this book is that story—my family's story, the same one I tell in "A Jew Grows in Brooklyn"—only without the music and the footlights. And yet it expands it, by chronicling the journey—dysfunction, humor, sadness, and all—that led me to where I am now.

But it's not only about *my* family and *my* experiences—it's about *your* story, too, because our shared journey of life holds the same basic challenges: Challenges of fear and perseverance, of finding beauty and love, of searching for meaning, and of learning that we are so much more than just our circumstances. And if we have a few laughs and lessons along the way, so much the better.

My family arrived in America in 1949—survivors of the Nazi Holocaust that ravaged the Jews and many others during World War II. Unlike their eight brothers and sisters, my parents survived the war by escaping to Russian work camps in Siberia, where my eldest sister Wanda was born. Shortly after the war, Joanie, my other sister, was born in a displaced persons camp in Germany. And me? Well, I was born in Brooklyn—a true-blue "Yankee Doodle," destined to tell the story for my family who is now gone. Or perhaps I should say *"Yonkee"* Doodle, because I was endearingly called by my Yiddish nickname "Yonkee" (Yankele) as a boy. I tried every which way to get rid of it, along with my family's history, and just fit in. All I wanted was to be a sure-fired, smack-damn, 100-percent, through-and-through, standard-issue, red-blooded American kid. Fitting in was a big deal for me. (Now, not so much.)

The story of my name is only one of many I want to share with you. Others include stories of my dad who worked seven days a week and our extraordinary relationship and his courageous battle with Parkinson's disease . . . of overcoming drug abuse . . . of being a musician living the rock-'n'-roll lifestyle . . . of my bachelor's obsession with women (that's a good one) . . . of learning to turn adversity into opportunity . . . of realizing that I was funny (yeah, well, we'll see) . . . of the incredible joys and challenges of parenting and marriage . . . of the continuing journey of self-discovery . . . and of the beautiful reactions I have had to my story—from people in all walks of life.

Stories of life and family history have been with us throughout recorded time. They teach, explain, and entertain. My intention is to offer you, through these stories, some glimpses of the attitudes and behaviors I've adopted that have played a part in my growth and success, both professionally and personally. I have, in great part, learned these lessons from others, and I hope, in turn, you will take away at least one lesson, or many, that will serve you and yours on your journey.

This book is about the quintessential *American* experience—the immigrant experience. Yet, on a deeper level it is about our common *human* experience, how we approach the inescapable adversity, tragedy, and challenges that life serves up, and how we ultimately find our way to the triumph or defeat of our soul and spirit. It's about choosing to define our circumstances in an empowering way and about learning to apply our focus and energy in a manner that serves us well. It's about living fruitfully and joyously and fully. It's about renewal—of spirit and body and mind. *(Wow, I'd like to read this book myself! Will it wash my car? Can it core "a" apple?)*

I hope that traveling these roads with me, not only gets you laughing and thinking, but inspires you to take a look back at the people and events that have been pivotal in your own life. Think about them, write them down, and share them with friends and family. Perhaps recalling your stories (maybe in a writing group or a book club—wait, *definitely* in a book club!) and discovering what you've learned might inspire others—or maybe just yourself.

With intention and faith, anything is possible. With love and joy and gratitude and an indomitable spirit, we can live our dreams and have a positive, lasting influence on the world and those around us.

So, on with the show. . . .

YONKEE
(or What's in a Name?)

"The meaning of things lies not in the things themselves,
but in our attitude towards them."

—Antoine de Saint Exupery

ON MY BLOCK OF TWO- AND THREE-family homes in the lower middle-class Brooklyn neighborhood where I grew up, my friends and I spent many glorious, carefree hours playing punch-ball, stickball, and box baseball with our ever-present pink "spawldeen" (Spalding) ball in hand. We played in the "gutter" and used the manhole covers for bases and landmarks, and if any car dared to interrupt our game by driving down our street, one or two of us would shout, "Hey, ya bums, go down Remsen Avenue, will ya!" Others would simply throw their hands up in the air and glare at the passing car.

Being there among my friends, the ball, and the manhole covers, I felt so all-American, so much a part of normal, everyday things that I was able to forget for a few hours just how different I felt.

At about five o'clock, we'd all get called in for dinner. Parents would simply shout their kids' names at the top of their lungs from the front porch or an open window. It would usually take them several tries before anyone really moved. Going home at the first call was a sign of wimpiness. Ignoring the call was a sign of coolness. So, the longer you waited, the cooler you were. Yelling back at the top of your lungs, *"Ten more minutes!"* was also deemed acceptable.

I would be minding my own business, playing with my friends—the picture of the cool American kid—when the calls would begin....

"Michael!"

"Steeeeven!"

"Gaaaary!"

"Joey!"

I knew my dreaded call was coming. I'd tense up and a knot would form in my stomach. I'd cringe in anticipation. Then, it would come, my mother's heavily accented English echoing down the street: "Yohnkeeeee!"

At that moment, the regular all-American kid would morph into "super-immigrant Jew kid with Holocaust-survivor parents." Of course I knew we were different—that I was different, even though I was born in the United States—but in those days, I simply didn't want to be different. I wanted to be like everyone else. I wanted to have "normal" parents like everyone else. But my mother would totally "out" me every time.

In 1949, my parents and two sisters, Joanie and Wanda, came to the United States from a displaced persons camp in Germany after World War II. I was born several years later.

As European Jewish tradition dictates, my parents named me after the deceased: their fathers. My paternal grandfather, Yankel Ehrenreich, died on Yom Kippur, the holiest day of the Jewish year, just before World War II. Mercifully, he didn't live to see the destruction of his family. My mom's dad, Yitzchak Chojnaska, perished in the Holocaust. Therefore, my given name is Jacob (Yankel) Isaac (Yitzchak) Ehrenreich after these two men. (I received both the American versions of their names as well as the Yiddish.) The responsibility that comes from carrying their names into the world fills me with bittersweet pride, and I try to do the names justice.

When I was young, my parents called me by my Yiddish name, "Yankele," which is the loving, diminutive form of Yankel. There's even a song by that title, which my mother sang to me as a lullaby when I was very small. In English it goes, "Sleep now, my precious son, and close your pretty eyes. Soon enough you'll be grown, but for a while you're still here with us. There will be much hard work and tears, before we make a mentsh of you."

Sure it's a lovely song, but since my childhood was defined by a fervent desire to be a regular American kid, it didn't take very long before Yankele was *not* what I wanted to be called in public. As a compromise, I opted for the vastly superior Yonkee. I even called myself "The Yonk," in keeping with the best tradition of adolescents who refer to themselves in the third person: *The Yonk hits a long fly ball to left . . . it drops in. . . . The Yonk is rounding third and headed for home . . . it's gonna be close . . . there's the throw. . . . The Yonk is safe at the plate!*

Ultimately, even Yonkee sounded just a bit "too Jewish" for my tastes. It's not that I was embarrassed to be Jewish. Most of my friends were. It was the whole immigrant scene that made me uncomfortable. The accents, the funny names, my parents' obvious cultural differences, our lack of an extended family . . . oh yeah, our lack of extended family—no grandparents, no aunts, no uncles, no cousins—the whole Holocaust thing. It hung over my family like a dark shadow. *How could I fit in and be like everybody else with a history like that?!*

But in many ways I did succeed at fitting in. I was popular, and I was good at all the games that guaranteed entry to the "in" crowd: baseball, basketball, football, punchball, and stickball. I was always picked near the top when choosing up sides for teams. By all outward appearances, I had the whole American thing pretty well in hand, yet I still felt like an outsider.

The older I got, the more I felt I needed a real American name. Even when I went from the Yiddish *Yonkee* on the street, to the English *Jacob* in school, it still didn't feel right. The first day of a new year of grade school would always start off the same. The teacher would call the role and my name would come up: "Jacob Errrchhrnrrcchhhnn. . . ." The other kids would laugh because my last name was difficult to pronounce, but the laughter didn't bother me. What bugged me was the "Jacob" part . . . too "Jewish," not "American." So I finally came up with my new American persona: "Jack."

Jack was a totally acceptable nickname for Jacob, and what could be more American than Jack . . . as in Jack Kennedy?! Jack was *it* and was *it* for many years to come. Even my folks began to call me Jack, but, of course, from them it sounded more like *Jeck.*

As a child, my father tried desperately to convey to me that fitting in was not always necessary or even desirable. Unfortunately, I was too immature to hear him. (I couldn't understand why *But EVERY-BODY'S doing it!* never won any battles with him.) Even as I got older, I played around with alternative names, some of my own making and some that were foisted upon me by others in the entertainment industry. "Jack Allyn" was a bandleader name I received. I chose "Jake Shephard" for a week as a stand-up comedian in Aruba. I toyed with the name "Jac Renik," but that sounded too robotic. And I actually used "Jake the Snake" for a while with my rock band. That lasted until a guy showed up at a gig threatening to beat me up if he didn't get his money back. He was expecting to see "Jake the Snake" the popular wrestler. *Who Knew?* Overall, I think the name that takes the prize was "Jackson Woods." It just made me sound like a Black R & B singer.

When I was in my thirties, I landed a role in the Off-Broadway show *The Golden Land*, which was about Jewish immigration to America. Since I took the job as homage to my parents and my heritage, it seemed the perfect place to use my given name. For the first time in my life, I told everyone my name was Jacob.

That's when the director who had also directed "Oh! Calcutta!" and produced records with Bob Dylan—*um, how exactly did he get this gig?*—decided to call me Jake. As it turns out, "Jake" stuck. And I'm actually pleased with it, but what's in a name anyhow?

To some, a name can be extraordinarily important—to their identity and even to their self-worth. It was for me as a kid, but the truth is more complicated. I was stressing about just the right name to call myself because I didn't know who I really was. I was conflicted and uncomfortable over my role as an American, a pseudo-immigrant, a Holocaust-survivor kid, a Jew . . . you name it. My desire to fit in as a boy, my misperception of what it meant to be American, and my own insecurity led me to be uncomfortable with a perfectly good name.

Ralph Waldo Emerson said, "What you are shouts so loudly in my ears that I cannot hear what you say." And it's true. Each of us exudes an internal comfort or discomfort, which others detect on a deep, subconscious level. I learned that the challenge in life is to find a path to be internally comfortable in general—with our name, our dress, and ultimately ourselves.

A few years ago, I walked into a friend's leather shop to pick out a coat. I went with the intent to purchase something, but I couldn't find anything I liked. As we were saying our good-byes, I noticed a magnificent Native American–style jacket hanging on the wall behind his desk. It was hand-embroidered leather, complete with turquoise and leather fringe. It was simply stunning, albeit very unusual.

"Hey, what's that?" I asked.

"Oh, that?!" he said. "That's a great jacket, but no one has the balls to wear it, so I hung it as a piece of art."

I asked him to take it down and slipped it on. It fit as though it were custom made for me, and it felt like a second skin. The weight of it on my body was like a challenge from the universe: "I dare you."

"I'll take it!" I said, with much anticipation and excitement.

Now, there are days when I can wear that jacket and days when I cannot. Whenever I choose to wear it, it garners *a lot* of attention, even in Manhattan, where you can have two heads and barely warrant a second look. When I'm feeling confident in it, I get all sorts of complimentary looks and comments. (If I were still single, I'd be wearing it *a lot* on those days.) When I'm not feeling confident in it, people just look at me like I'm some kind of schmuck. The difference is *how I feel in my skin.*

As a kid, I just wanted to fit in, but I truly didn't know what that meant. My name was uncomfortable simply because *I* was uncomfortable in it. Doing our best to live a confident, well-balanced, authentic life free from shame gives us the best shot at fitting in anywhere, at anytime. I might have learned that lesson long ago had I listened to my dad.

What I've discovered about myself over the years is that my story *is* the quintessential American story. Being an American is, by definition, being a "child" of immigrants. Our experience of life is based on our own perception of what is true and what we choose to focus on. I've found that I am many things, and they are not contradictory. In fact, the sum of my parts makes me stronger. Today, there is nothing I like more than hearing a childhood friend call me Yonkee.

As a child, I changed my name. As an adult, I changed myself.

THE ALKA-SELTZER BOTTLES
(or "It Was Me. I Took the Coins.")

*"I think a dysfunctional family is any family
with more than one person in it."*

—Jerry Seinfeld

WE HAD SO MUCH ALKA-SELTZER in my childhood home that I thought it was some sort of obscure Jewish dietary thing. Turns out, it was for my dad's intense stomach ulcer, which he had lived with for many, many years. For those of you uninitiated in the joys of Alka-Seltzer, let me give you a better description of this much sought after elixir of modern medicine. Picture the original movie version of *The Strange Story of Dr. Jekyll and Mr. Hyde* starring Spencer Tracy and a scorchingly hot nineteen-year-old Ingrid Bergman. (Alternatively, you may choose any old movie featuring a mad scientist, but personally I'm sticking with the Ingrid Bergman thing.) You know that smoking, bubbling, churning, turn me into Mr. Hyde–concoction that Dr. Jekyll mixes up in his lab? That's Alka-Seltzer.

If you combine my dad's ongoing relationship with the aforementioned Alka-Seltzer with his inability to throw *anything* away, you could find yourself accumulating an astonishingly large stash of empty Alka-Seltzer bottles. And we did.

It is a well-documented scientific fact (well, not really) that Holocaust survivors and their children were the original recyclers; we hang on to *everything*. We simply don't throw anything away. I still have assorted piles of unused wood, decking, wires, pipes, and the odd lawn chair lying around my yard. Amazingly, my wife doesn't mind! (And I know of a bridge for sale, too.) I think the worst moment came when my brother-in-law started whistling the theme from *Sanford and Son* as he approached my front porch.

Sweetheart, it's good stuff . . . I'll make something out of it may have sounded sweet when my wife, Lisa, and I were dating, but somewhere along the line, the novelty of marrying a *handy* Jewish guy seems to have worn off.

I come by my rat-packedness honestly. When I was a kid, my morning orange juice glass was the leftover glass from a used yahrtzeit candle. For those of you unfamiliar, a yahrtzeit candle is a glass filled with wax and a wick, designed to burn for twenty-four hours, which is traditionally lit in honor of the dead on the anniversary of their passing. Recycling a yahrtzeit glass like this must have been truly unique, because I even get looks of disbelief from other survivor-family friends when I tell them about this. (And my mother wondered why I didn't like orange juice.)

My dad, who was always very inventive in the ways of recycling stuff (my favorites were building fences out of old steel bed frames and wearing my old clothes, which he called "hand me ups"), invented a great use for the leftover Alka-Seltzer bottles. Sometime in the early to mid-1970s, the U.S. Mint announced that they would no longer be minting dimes and quarters in full silver. The new coins would contain copper in their centers, a much less expensive material. Being a thoughtful and forward-looking chap, my dad figured the full silver coins would be worth something extra in the future (he was right), so he started to collect these coins in a convenient, economical, and readily available storage system: the empty Alka-Seltzer bottles.

This whole scheme was pretty ingenious. He stored the bottles of coins in his desk hutch (which he never locked—*oops*), and the coins were kept neat and safe for a rainy day. As kids, we were always told to check our coins, and he would trade us some non-silver coins in return for any we found. Dimes and quarters only; pennies are made of copper and nickels are made of . . . well, nickel (I guess).

Many years later, when he hit a bad stretch, my dad sold the coins to Lefty of the famous Lefty's Restaurant in Monticello, New York. As dad tells it, he didn't get what they were worth, but he was in a bind, so he had to sell. I always felt bad when he told that story, because when I was growing up, I would periodically "borrow" some of the coins from his precious silver coin stash. The whole forgetting-to-lock-your-desk thing was a huge mistake. I was fifteen years old and strapped for cash!

I wasn't greedy. I would take only a few coins at a time, and that somehow made it feel less like stealing. Only once did I actually go into my dad's pants and pull out a twenty-dollar bill, but that was an emergency. I had lost a bet with Jeffrey Feinstein that I could "punch" a *spawldeen* over the fence at Ditmas Park. Although I had done this a trillion times before, I totally choked. After going double or nothing a few times, I ended up owing him fourteen dollars. I heard he was looking for me, and Feinstein was tough!

What was really astounding is that, even though I would take only a few coins at a time (and from different bottles), somehow my dad knew! He would come to dinner and ask if anyone was taking coins, because he seemed to be missing some.

What?! This was a man who would leave his car keys on the dining room table overnight with an out-of-control teenage son in the house. I would take his car out at 2 AM and go to the Foursome Diner on Avenue U with my two crazy sisters, Joanie and Wanda, and then park the car in a different place when I returned home. He never even noticed! And now he somehow knew that I took a total of four dimes and three quarters out of seven different jars, in a desk that had dozens? *Impossible!* I'd seen *Twilight Zone* episodes that required less of a stretch. Of course, I categorically denied any knowledge of the affair.

Fast-forward about twenty-five years. We're having dinner at my dad's house. The evening includes my sisters, my dad, his wife Ruth,* and me. It was an unusual evening in that things were actually going pretty well and we were all getting along. This was *extremely* rare, especially between my dad and my sister Wanda. We were making the most out of the occasion by telling some old tried-and-true stories of our dysfunctional family, and we were actually having a few laughs about it. (A rare night indeed.) Out of the blue, my sister Joanie announced she had a confession to make.

"Hey, dad," she began. "Remember you thought someone was taking coins from the Alka-Seltzer bottles in your desk?"

He looked at her quizzically and nodded.

"It was me!" she confessed.

This was a shocker. Joanie was the Goody Two–Shoes of the

---

*See author's note on page 17.

family. She was the only one of the three of us who'd ever been well behaved in school. We were dumbfounded, but before any of us could respond, she went on.

"I felt guilty about it, but I was afraid to tell you, so I told Mommy instead. She told me not to feel too bad because she was taking the coins, too!"

My father was speechless. I opened my mouth to confess my own guilt, but before I could get a word out, Wanda chimed in, "What do you mean it was you? It was me! I took the coins!"

What?! No wonder he knew! My whole cleptomaniac family was taking money from my poor trusting father! It was like our own little Brooklyn-Jew-crime syndicate.

By the time I added that I'd been taking the coins, too, my sisters and I were laughing pretty hard. My father seemed like he could care less. I guess with all the trouble he'd been through in his life, and more recently with my mom's early-onset Alzheimer's disease, this admission was not something to get worked up about. (At the time, my sisters were still pretty okay, if you could call their lives okay, but they would also succumb to early-onset Alzheimer's disease.)

What's ironic about the fact we were taking the coins from under my father's nose is that when we were growing up, he was fond of saying, "Are you trying to make a fool out of me?" Poor guy, turns out we were. (I guess this goes to show us that we should be careful of what we focus on.) In truth, we never intended to make a fool of my dad. We were just a slightly off-balance family (well, maybe slightly more than slightly), but none of this was ever meant to be malicious.

Ruth was the only one who was upset that evening. She thought we were laughing at my father. This shocked me. Couldn't she see how much I loved my father? She knew how close we were and that I'd never do anything to hurt him. This was simply a long-ago story, from a galaxy far, far away, and it had no power left. I explained to Ruth that we were not laughing *at* my dad; we were simply sharing a lighthearted moment together as a family, which was very rare and precious to us. If this dysfunctional memory is what it took for us to create a new fond memory of being together, then so be it.

My father wasn't much fazed by our admission of guilt. He eventually bought into the spirit of the evening and came to see the humor in it. He knew the score. In the literal madness of our lives, with the years of illness and sadness and loneliness, it was a true blessing for us to be able to laugh together.

They say that crime doesn't pay, but it did that night, because it brought us closer together.

AUTHOR'S NOTE: *My mom had died some years earlier after being institutionalized with early-onset Alzheimer's disease for many years. Ruth Sussman had attended a Yiddish class my dad was teaching, and they had much in common. She was also taking care of a spouse with Alzheimer's disease, she spoke Yiddish, and much more. . . . They spent many happy years together. In fact, Ruth, who is an organic vegetarian, totally changed my dad's life by altering his diet and offering him unconditional love. When he became ill, she cared for him unselfishly and without limits. She became part of the family, and she is my son's* bubbe *(grandma) who now lives right next door to us on the lake. She is ninety years old and is on no medication. She works out every day, swims in the lake during the summer, and is a great babysitter! We love you, Bubbe!*

THROUGH THE WINDOW ...

(or You May Be the World to Someone)

"The best things in life aren't things."

—Art Buchwald

THERE ARE SOME THINGS in life we don't quite appreciate until we are older—or at least not until we've had a similar experience ourselves. Now that I'm a father, some shared experiences with my own dad have taken on a much deeper meaning.

My dad suffered with debilitating stomach ulcers for many years. On a few occasions, I could hear him crying through the locked bathroom door. As my father was not prone to crying—or showing his soft side much at all during my childhood years—hearing him like that was frightening and confusing.

After many years of intense suffering, my dad finally relented to the doctors' recommendation that he undergo a very serious ulcer operation. In fact, they would cut out half his stomach. Medical advances have made this approach obsolete in many cases, and oftentimes, stomach ulcers can now be treated with a course of antibiotics.

I was young at the time, maybe eight or nine, and I guess I didn't fully appreciate the gravity of the situation. But my dad's missing work was a *very big* deal, so I must have understood at least a little that it was somewhat serious. I mean, he basically worked seven days a week for at least fifteen years. My sisters and I didn't see him much in those days, and as much as I wanted to just be free to do my own thing, I would have *loved* to have him around more. In fact, one of Wanda's dates got totally spooked when he met my dad at the house one evening—later, he told her he just assumed her father was dead.

When he was much older and we'd grown close, my dad told me he regretted working such long hours when we were kids. He'd believed his role was to provide for the family, and my mother's role was to raise the kids, which was a traditional belief at the time. Unfortunately, he eventually came to understand that in many ways my mother was ill suited to the task, but by then we were practically grown.

Anyhow, the day came when my dad went off to the hospital. He would be there for a few days to prep before the operation. The day before the surgery was to take place, my dad asked for me to visit him that morning. This confused me, because I'd already been told that I was too young to visit my dad at the hospital. My mom explained that, although I couldn't go inside, I could stand in the parking lot below my dad's window and he could see me from there for our "visit." *Huh?!*

It's possible I might have found this scenario more reasonable if I didn't have a *huge* baseball game with my friends scheduled for the same time. If I could really visit him, that would be one thing, but it didn't seem worth it to miss the Big Game just to wave to each other from the window. I thought that would be really lame. Besides, what's the big deal? He'd be home from the hospital in just a few days, wouldn't he?

After much discussion, I ended up *not* going to the hospital that day. Of course, now I'm quite certain my decision must have broken my father's heart. To make matters worse, I later learned my dad believed he had a good chance of dying "under the knife" while in surgery. He loved me so much that he simply wanted to look at me for what he thought might be the last time. I can't even imagine how disappointed and afraid he must have been. Only now, as the father of a young boy myself, can I fully appreciate how seeing your child under these circumstances, even at a great distance, would be the most wonderful gift in the world.

I still feel shame and embarrassment at my behavior, even though it was so long ago. *How could I be so selfish? Why didn't my mother and sisters force me to go? How was my dad able to forgive me?*

I look back in wonder at some of the choices we make in life. I was a young boy, so I cut myself some slack, but I believe I was old enough to know the difference between right and wrong. Deep inside, I must have known my behavior was selfish.

Thank goodness my dad survived; I know I never would have forgiven myself if he hadn't. We went on to have an extremely rewarding and fulfilling father/son relationship—one that I've been told has been an inspiration and a model to many who knew us.

I've tried to learn from that long-ago experience, and I do my best to be there for family and friends. Sometimes we get only one bite at the apple. I was fortunate to get more. Perhaps that recital or parent-teacher conference or the tae kwon do test or soccer game doesn't seem so important to us. But it just could be very important to our child, or spouse . . . or parent. I figure it's best to err on the side of caution in these matters—better to be too available, than not at all.

Most of us need one another's love and support more than we admit. I know how different special events feel to me when my family's there, and I've seen the disappoint-ment even in my wife Lisa's eyes the few times I've been unable to attend some function or other with her. It's easy to rationalize not being there—there'll be another time—*but only if we're lucky.*

A Mother's Day plaque that our son, Dovy, bought for Lisa perhaps sums it up best. It reads: TO THE WORLD, YOU MAY BE JUST ONE PERSON, BUT TO ONE PERSON YOU MAY JUST BE THE WORLD.

AUTHOR'S NOTE: *I so much wanted to use a photo of me and my dad from this time of my life, but given his long hours of work, there simply are none. My son and I will have to fit the bill.*

THE CHINESE LOTS
(or Another Broken Window)

"Life isn't a matter of milestones, but of moments."

—Rose Kennedy

I SPENT MOST OF MY CHILDHOOD in the East Flatbush section of Brooklyn, having moved there from Brownsville when I was about five years old. My memories of what we called the "old neighborhood" in Brownsville are sketchy, but I still recall the excitement in the summertime when the older kids would open up the fire hydrants and we'd all splash around in the rushing water. In later years, we'd sometimes drive through "the old neighborhood" on the way to my dad's store. It looked like Dresden after the war—which is to say, many of the buildings and stores were boarded up and closed, and the place seemed wild and forsaken. That's not how I remembered it, and it was unsettling to me that things could change like that. (I had a similar feeling many years later in the Catskill Mountains when seeing the decaying hotels and bungalow colonies of my youth.)

As we approached our new neighborhood, we would drive by the Dime Savings Bank, which we called the "shiny" bank because of its unique exterior. It made me feel better to see that was still okay.

The "new neighborhood" of East Flatbush was a working lower middle-class area made up of mostly Jewish families, with a smattering of Italian, Irish, Black, and Hispanic families thrown in.

My elementary school, PS 233, was about six blocks to the east and my junior high and high school—Meyer Levin Junior High School and Samuel J. Tilden High School—were about eight blocks to the south. All of the schools were within walking distance, so that's how I got to and from school. It is inconceivable to me now, but even as a small child, I walked to school alone and also went home every day for lunch. Most parents these days would think letting a little kid walk all alone to school is crazy.

The school yard and park were off limits when I was very young, because the older, tougher kids hung out there. We usually just played on our street, but there was one very special place we called all our own: it wasn't a school yard, park, or street. It was the Chinese Lots, and it was *very* important to us.

The Chinese Lots was a large dirt area about the size of a football field, perhaps a bit longer, but not as wide. It was the back lot to several stores and factories, and one of those stores was the Mayflower Chinese Restaurant—hence the name we called the area: "The Chinese Lots."

Since grass yards were not the norm in our area of Brooklyn, it was the only unpaved area to play in, and we took full advantage of it. We'd build forts out of old cardboard and discarded pieces of wood. (Stuff was always getting dumped in the lots, and we creatively used whatever we could find to build these forts.) We'd have rock-throwing fights with the forts as protection, and sometimes we'd just hang out in them for hours. It was a miracle that we made our way around the broken bottles, rusty nail-ridden boards, and other trash without getting seriously hurt. I loved the freedom and the mystery of the back area where a few overgrown bushes and small trees grew. To me, it was like being in the woods. I was practically an adolescent Thoreau. My friend Gary Rosen's dad, Ira, would play a baseball game called "pepper" with us in the lots. Ira Rosen was a real American dad. He had a pretty wife and owned two of the greatest cars of all time: the classic T-Bird and the Lincoln Continental with the cool doors they now use in the opening credits of the TV show *Entourage*. While my dad was busy working, Gary's dad was always doing stuff with us. He even taught me to ride a bike and took me to my first live baseball game. (In later years, my dad expressed regret over missing out on things like that.)

By contrast, my father didn't even understand the game of baseball. To be fair, it wasn't a popular game in pre–World War II Poland where he grew up. I recall watching our first televised baseball game together. It was a great pitcher's duel; no score, very few hits. About the fifth or sixth inning, my dad turned to me and in his thick European accent said, "What kind of game is this baseball? Two people play and eight people watch." It was still cool, though, because we were watching the game together as father and son, which to me was a very American thing to do.

As we got a bit older, we used the Chinese Lots mostly as a baseball field. Invariably someone would hit a foul ball and break a window in the back of one of the buildings. Instead of staying and owning up to what we'd done, our reaction was to simply run for it. I always felt bad about it, but it was truly exhilarating when that happened, and I felt totally alive. It was a huge adrenaline rush to run out of there with total abandon—frightened and laughing at the same time. As you can imagine, this really pissed off the store owners, and they tried all sorts of ways to stop us from playing there. *Good luck.*

One Sunday, when I was about ten, my dad was scheduled to work only half a day, which was a very rare occurrence. I went out to play in the lots and agreed to come back early so we could spend some time together, just the two of us. I didn't know exactly what we would do, but I had a suspicion we'd probably work on the white picket fence he wanted to build around the front of our house—not my idea of a good time. Sure enough, someone hit a long foul ball . . . *SMASH!* You could hear the glass breaking a block away. As usual, we all scurried out of there as fast as we could—except this time, I was not so lucky.

I was playing the field adjacent to the driveway that led to the street. By some terrible stroke of misfortune, the owner of the building whose window we'd just broken was already headed down the driveway to kick us out. I ran as fast as I could, but to no avail. In no time, he had me in his clutches.

This was probably about the tenth window of his we had broken. I was terrified. I don't remember precisely what happened, but I do remember he roughed me up a bit. I'm sure it was nothing serious; he probably just intended to put a good scare into me. When he finally let me go, I was sobbing pretty heavily, more out of fear than of actually being hurt.

I ran back to my house as fast as I could. By the time I arrived home, I had calmed down a bit, but I was still shaken up. It was at that moment I realized how late I was getting home. I was definitely in trouble. Had this been the first time, it might have been different, but

I was *always* late getting home. Not only that, somehow in the heat of the game, I totally forgot my dad was coming home early. This was *not* going to be good.

Just as I was about to go in, inspiration struck. I was already upset, so it didn't take much for me to drum up some extra tears and emotion when I recounted the story of my trauma. I kept it simple. *I was playing in the Chinese Lots. Some man didn't want us there. He chased me and hit me.* I conveniently left out the part about the broken window.

My plan worked perfectly. After hearing my story, my father wasn't even angry with me. In fact, he was very understanding! On the other hand, he did seem pretty angry with the guy who had roughed me up. I guess the idea of an adult (other than himself) hitting his young son sent him over the edge. I had never quite seen him so freaked out like that before. He seemed strangely calm but really intense.

I definitely didn't plan on what happened next. Before I knew it, he took me by the arm and led me out of the house. He wanted me to take him to find this man.

A thousand thoughts rushed through my little adolescent brain as we marched down the street. *When my dad finds out we broke this guy's window, he'll kill me! When he finds out how many windows we broke before that, he'll raise me from the dead so he can kill me again! When the guy says he didn't really hit me (which was sort of true), I'll have to fess up, and then he'll kill me for real!*

But, by far, the foremost thought in my mind had to do with my dad's safety. The man who shook me up was a young, burly, tough guy. My dad was maybe five-foot-six-inches tall on a good day and not in the best of health. Unless he had been secretly studying martial arts instead of going to work every day, this could be really, really bad. Now, the guilt began welling up in me, and I was crying pretty heavily. *What if my father gets beat up because of me?* About a block before we reached the Chinese Lots, I made my decision.

"Daddy . . . I lied."

We came to an abrupt halt. He looked down at me.

"What do you mean?" he asked.

"I made up the whole story," I confessed between sobs. I told him it was all just an excuse I invented to get out of trouble for coming home late. *Holy Toledo, did I just say that?* I thought.

My dad's anger shifted quite suddenly. Honestly, what came directly after my partial confession is sort of a blur. I'm sure he must have wacked me, though. Lying was a *huge* deal. But I think his anger was partially fueled by relief, as in when I would get home really late and my parents would hit me while just being happy that I was still alive: "Thank God you're alright!" *Wham!*

It didn't really bother me that I was in big trouble. Mostly, I felt relieved that my dad wouldn't get beat up, and I was really proud that I had protected him, as he had been willing to protect me. In all likelihood, my dad was probably thrilled that he didn't have to confront this guy, who might have been Bruno Sammartino for all he knew. Yet he was willing to stand up to him anyhow. For my part, I'll never forget how proud and protected I felt.

As a boy, this day became my own little secret, and I felt proud of what I'd done for a long time. It was the least I could do, not fully disclosing that the guy *had* roughed me up, considering what my dad was willing to risk for me. And it was certainly a more exciting afternoon than working on that sad white picket fence he wanted me to help him build . . . *with only hand tools!*

Later in life, I never talked to my dad about what happened that day— for no other reason than because I didn't think of bringing it up. But now I wonder how he would have remembered that day—if at all. It is times like these, when I want to turn to my dad and say something like, "Hey, dad, remember when . . ." that I miss him most. I'll never forget that day, and I'll remember it for the both of us.

AUTHOR'S NOTE: *I mention a few times that my sisters and I got "hit" by my parents. In my mind, this was never intended to do real physical harm. It was intended to teach a lesson, and I clearly understood that as a child. This was simply a normal part of life in Eastern Europe (even in the schools they attended). Although I don't condone or practice this type of discipline with my own family, I want to point out the distinction between a literal "beating" and the occasional smack or two (or three) that we sometimes received. This punishment was not frequent in our home and only happened in response to our behavior. In later years, I would tell my dad that if he tried that stuff today, concerned neighbors would call child protective services. My dad and I would have a little laugh, but I clearly saw that he was always a bit embarrassed by this behavior.*

CASTRO CONVERTIBLES
(or Only in the Mind of a Child)

"Truly wonderful, the mind of a child is."

—Yoda

NOW THAT I'M A FATHER, I often wonder how my son's brain works. *What is he thinking? What is important to him? What's going on in his imagination? What does he worry about?* I sometimes try to remember how I used to think when I was a boy and perhaps gain some insight from those memories about what my son, Dovy, is thinking.

I noticed pretty early on that when Dovy asked a question, I was always better off giving him a real answer than to fudge it or say, "You wouldn't understand." Avoiding an issue only resulted in his asking more and different questions. If I gave him a good answer, even one he couldn't yet understand, he seemed satisfied that I had attempted to answer him honestly. I liked his attitude and was happy to have an intelligent, inquisitive boy. I tried to encourage his desire for knowledge and let him know that I was a safe place to go to for information. Unfortunately, I didn't have that opportunity growing up.

I guess since my dad worked so much and my mom was kind of confused, I ended up making my own sense of the things I didn't fully comprehend. For instance, I thought cats were girls, and dogs were boys, and I can still understand the thought process that led me to that conclusion. By far, however, the biggest mystery in my early life had to do with something known as the Castro Convertible. The Castro Convertible Company was one of the first sofa bed companies in New York and perhaps in the nation. The sofas were extremely popular, and the company ran frequent TV commercials that featured a very catchy jingle, which made several claims about the product. The foremost of which were that Castro Convertibles . . .

1. Were the first to conquer living space
2. Conquered space with fine design
3. Saved you money all the time

As I said, they ran this commercial a *lot*! Anyone who grew up in the New York area in the 1960s who watched TV would be all too familiar with this ad. Castro Convertibles and their ever-present commercials were both confusing and frightening to me.

I must have been about seven years old at the time these commercials aired, and I was only vaguely aware of the world events taking place around me. Like most kids, I seemed to know only bits and pieces of what was going on without fully understanding the whole picture or context. A good example of this was when President Kennedy was shot. I was in the second grade. We were sent home from school early that day, but before we left, I had been on an errand to the mimeograph machine (or was it a rexograph machine?!). Although I couldn't make out everything they were saying, I overheard some teachers whispering in the hallway about "President Kennedy" and "shot in the head." All the way home from school that day, I wondered what terrible thing someone might have done that President Kennedy would order him to be shot in the head. It didn't seem right somehow. Of course, when I got home, I learned the terrible truth, but it goes to show that kids are quite capable of mixing things up a bit.

Let me set the stage of world events at about the time I was watching those offending and frightening TV commercials:

1. Fidel Castro had been in the news rather frequently, especially regarding the then-recent Cuban missile crisis.
2. We were locked in an adversarial nuclear arms race with the Russians.
3. We were deeply involved in a competitive and none-too-friendly space race with the Russians.
4. I was aware that the Russians were somehow linked with Castro. (They were close military allies.)

And, for the purposes of fully understanding my mind-set, you should also know that:

5. My father was an upholsterer and owned a furniture store.

Okay, now the stage is set.

The first line of the jingle was enough to get me running under my desk for nuclear cover. *"The first to conquer living space, it's the Castro Convertible."* What?! My kid brain interpreted this to mean that *space* had been *conquered by Castro*! Oh my God, we had lost the space race! And who was the *conqueror* of *space*? None other than *Castro*! Fidel Castro (the real-life Boris Badenov), who was also closely linked to the Ruskies and their nuclear weapons! *Disaster*! This was still in the era of the whole cold-war/nuclear-bomb/hide-under-your-desk world. I was a kid; I was terrified. What would happen? How could this be? We were the all powerful U. S. of A.! The next line really sent me over the top. *"Who conquers space with fine design and saves you money all the time."* This was cheerfully sung while an attractive young girl effortlessly opened up a convertible sofa bed in a living room full of beautiful furniture. This was awful! Not only did Castro and the Russians win the space race and *conquer space*, but to make matters worse, they were somehow in the furniture business. And they did it with *fine design* to boot! It seemed this fellow Castro had developed some space-age technology (probably when conquering outer space) for a couch that opened up into a bed! Holy Mackerel, these guys were my father's competitors!

Things looked bleak for us. For goodness sake, if these guys beat the entire United States of America into space, what chance did my poor sickly Holocaust-survivor father stand against them with his little furniture store in Brownsville? And, to add insult to injury, Castro was also a discounter! He *saved you money all the time*! Yet, even worse than all that, I noticed something in the ad that could change the whole *fabric* of life as we knew it. The sofa in the ad had *no plastic slipcovers on it*! I may have been a confused kid, but even I knew the whole plastic-slipcover thing was a loser and now the rest of the world would know, too!

This was an unmitigated disaster in my mind, and the commercial haunted me. It changed my entire life. Gone were the carefree days of watching early morning Saturday cartoons. I would wait in frightened anticipation for the dreaded commercial to come on. Then I would watch closely for any weakness I might discern. This was a huge leap from watching Charlie the Tuna get fan mail from some flounder. I felt quite alone in my fight to save America and my dad, because mysteriously, no one else seemed too worked up about the whole thing.

I never spoke to anyone about this (which is why I encourage my son to ask questions). For one, I certainly didn't want to demoralize my poor dad; he had enough problems. He worked so much and so hard, I figured he probably hadn't yet heard about what had happened. Far be it for me to tell him the bad news. Given the circumstances, he probably didn't have much time left with his little *fakakte* ("crummy") business. Let him enjoy his last days.

And for another, I figured everyone else was just resigned to the fact that we lost the space race and that Castro would be in charge. Believe me, if they were concerned, they sure seemed pretty nonchalant about it.

Somehow I went on with my everyday life. I think that's part of the miracle of being a kid. It's sort of like the violence in the Looney Tunes cartoons: Wile E. Coyote falls from cliffs, gets crushed by boulders, and blows himself up over and over again, yet somehow he walks away. Same thing with Daffy Duck who gets shot in the face (among many other despicable mishaps) and miraculously lives. In a way, it's a pretty cool world. No one gets hurt.

My son is older than I was then (he's eleven now), but I still think about how his brain works. Sometimes I'll pick him up from the school bus, and he'll seem in a sullen mood. I'll ask, "What's wrong?" The reply is invariably the same: "Nothing." Yet I can tell something

is up. *Did some kid hurt his feelings? Was he worried about me or Mommy? Was an adult insensitive?* (For instance, Dovy once told me that his art teacher told one of his classmates that his art-work looked like it was done by a two-year-old, and the kid started to cry.) Who knows what's transpired that day if he doesn't say?

If I miss one of his tae kwon do tests, and he says, "That's okay," does he really feel okay about it? (By the way, Dovy is now a black belt, and I rarely miss anything.) What goes through my son's head when my wife and I argue? He clearly doesn't like it. Does he think we'll get a divorce? He's never mentioned it, but some of his friends' parents have split up, so it can't be that far from his mind. We always reassure him after we have an argument by letting him see us work it out. We explain that even people who love each other can have mis-understandings or hurt feelings. The key is to make your case and see it through honestly, not to bottle it up. We just want him to know how to communicate. We tell him not to worry; we were simply too old when we got married to get a divorce, and he laughs.

I think it's safe to say that most of us were far more sensitive as chil-dren than we ever let on, and we can therefore recognize this sensitiv-ity in our own kids. Sometimes we simply can't know what our kids are thinking, and that's fine. But looking back on my life and recalling what it was like to be a kid and how my brain operated back then simply makes me more aware and approachable as a parent. All parents have the opportunity to create a safe place to encourage dialogue when our kids are ready to talk. Had I felt confident to ask a question about the whole Castro thing, I might have saved myself a *ton* of angst. When our son, Dovy, was born, we used a special *Midrash*—a traditional Jewish teaching—on his birth announcement. It read:

**"With each child,
the world begins anew."**

With the birth of my son, the world had begun anew, and I'm honored and happy to take this journey through childhood once again, this time with him, and recall a little of what I was like as a kid . . . just don't make me sleep on a sofabed.

TEACHERS
(or The Lesson Joe Taught Me)

"The greatest good you can do for another is not just to share your riches, but reveal to them their own."

—Benjamin Disraeli

TEACHERS IN OUR LIVES COME in all shapes and sizes, and most of us remember those special few who significantly affected us in our early years. Sometimes they were the teachers we had in school, but often they were simply people who took the extra time to teach a lesson to a young person just because it was the right thing to do.

As a young boy growing up in Brooklyn, I had many diverse jobs. I had a newspaper-delivery route, I shoveled snow in the winter, I was a delivery boy for a grocery store, I packed boxes at the local chain department store, and I worked as a salad man at a local Italian restaurant: La Croce Via.

Joe was the chef-owner of La Croce Via, an Italian immigrant who still retained a heavy accent from the old country. He was small in stature but huge in presence, and he worked as hard as anyone I had ever seen. In many ways, he reminded me a lot of my father.

One afternoon, I went to the restaurant looking for a job, and I met with Joe. I was about twelve years old at the time. You had to be sixteen years old and have working papers to get hired, but somehow I landed a job. I thought I might get a job as a busboy if I were lucky, but as it turned out, I was to be the salad man. My job would consist of preparing baked clams, bringing Joe live lobsters from the walk-in freezer, making antipasto plates, and generally doing whatever anyone in the kitchen needed help with. This was a huge job for a young boy, and it put me in the kitchen with adults. Many of these were brand-new immigrants—"just off the boat" from Italy—and they spoke very little English.

Once, a dishwasher almost knifed me because I couldn't figure out what he was asking for. He had called me over and asked me for "abubulawada." As many times as I asked him to repeat what he wanted, I had absolutely no clue what he was saying. Finally, he just started shouting over and over "abubulawada!" "abubulawada!" "abubulawada!" He was sweating profusely from the heat in the kitchen, and now he was so angry, purple veins were popping out of his temples.

When the dishwasher reached for a kitchen knife—presumably to kill me with—the assistant cook stepped in. It was pretty frightening to me, but it was great entertainment for the rest of the kitchen staff, who were falling over themselves with laughter. When everyone calmed down a bit, someone asked him what he wanted in Italian.

As it turned out, "abubulawada" was seltzer or "bubbly water." Of course. Now it actually made sense. I secretly wondered if I could have done any better asking for seltzer in Italian. I guess we both felt a little bad about it, because he and I always liked each other after that.

Being a young kid, I was always the butt of jokes in the kitchen, but I just brushed it off. It was nice to have these guys treat me as one of their own. We were always laughing and having fun, even though we all worked very hard. In addition to earning my salary, I earned two meals every night. When I arrived at work after school, I would get the most delicious meatball hero sandwich ever. (Things just don't seem to taste that good anymore.) At the end of the evening, I would get my choice of dinner. When Joe would ask what I wanted to eat, the whole kitchen staff would come alive with suggestions. "How about trying some *[insert Italian-sounding word here]*." Of course, I had no idea what the words meant, so I would innocently ask, "Is that good?" Then everyone would keel over in hysterics.

I'm quite certain that if I'd paid closer attention, I could have learned all of the Italian words for the male and female genitalia (as well as some other choice words). The staff never seemed to tire of the laugh fest inspired by my dinner order, and I never ended up getting any real suggestions. I'd always have veal parmigiana. (If there is such a thing as Jewish Italian food, it's veal parmigiana.)

Anyhow, my lesson came the night Joe asked me to go to the basement and bring up a cheesecake. These were beautiful, creamy, homemade Italian cheesecakes that still make my mouth water when I think about them. On that night, I slipped on the greasy stairs leading up from the cellar and dropped the cake. Fortunately, I wasn't hurt, just a little bruised. I looked at the mess, and I panicked. Joe took great pride in getting only the best cheesecakes, and I knew how valuable they were—a cake like this would be cut into twenty dessert servings, and he had trusted me with it. Although I knew I should tell Joe, I was just too frightened and confused. He was a kind man, but he was also very strict. I decided I would cover my tracks as best as I could. With a racing heart, I cleaned up the formerly beautiful cake and stuffed it into the bottom of the large commercial waste container we used for restaurant trash. I was careful to cover it with other garbage, and I quickly got another cake and brought it up to Joe. I was pretty shaken up, but I somehow managed not to let it show—or at least that's what I thought.

When I arrived for work the next day, Joe immediately came over to me and led me down to the cellar. With each step down, the heat of shame crept further up my skin. Joe had somehow figured out what I had done and had retrieved the remains of the cake from the garbage, which he now held in his work-worn hands.

"Did you do this?" he asked.

"Yes," I replied, avoiding his disappointed gaze.

I didn't know how he found out, and I was scared—but in a way, I was relieved, too. I was sure I would lose my job, but the guilt had been weighing on me ever since the incident happened, and I was glad to have it out in the open.

"Why didn't you tell me?" he asked.

To my surprise, although Joe's attitude was quite serious, he didn't seem very angry with me at all. The feeling was vaguely reminiscent of my experience when I told my dad I'd been hit by that guy in the Chinese Lots.

I explained to Joe that I'd been too afraid to tell him that I had dropped the cheesecake because I didn't know what he would do.

Joe was magnificent. He patiently explained to me that a man must be responsible for his actions even when he doesn't know what the consequences of those actions might be. He told me that anyone can make a mistake and if I had told him about it when it had occurred, there would have been no penalty. He went on to explain that he would not fire me, but he felt I needed to learn an important lesson; therefore, he would take the cost of the cake out of my salary. Not all at once, but a little each week until it was paid off. I would still get a good paycheck. I cried a bit, but Joe didn't make any comment about my tears. That stood out to me because I was a sensitive kid, and I sometimes cried when my father reprimanded me as well. My dad thought it was weak for a boy to cry, so he would say, "You're crying? I'll give you something to cry about!" and then he'd whack me. (In retrospect, probably not the best parenting choice.) I cried during these times just to let out the emotion and because I was disappointed in myself.

Good to his word, Joe took a little money out each week—not too much, but just enough to make me notice.

This event had a profound effect on me, and still does. As a direct result of that experience, I've never felt the need to hide honest mistakes, and I try never to impose unfair consequences for unintended mishaps. I try to impress upon my son the importance of admitting one's errors and paying the consequences—they are usually less dire than we imagine, and telling the truth has rewards all its own. The greatest teacher is the feeling of experiencing one of these moments.

I absolutely consider Joe a hero, albeit unsung until now. I don't even know his last name, but I know he took time out of his busy life and business to teach a young boy an important life lesson. And I know the effect it's had on my life, and those I touch. As is usually the case, our deeds have ripples far beyond anything we can ever imagine.

I still have a vision in my head of the night my whole family came to eat at the restaurant shortly after the cake incident. I was working in the kitchen, and I felt proud and excited to know my family was out in the "house." Yet, this was a rare and somewhat confusing occasion. My father almost never arrived home before 9:00 PM, he practically *never* ate dinner out, and, if he did, he would *certainly* never eat Italian food because of his ulcer. What was even more unusual was that my dad asked to speak with Joe after dinner. I was not privy to the discussion between them, and as Joe was the main chef in this busy restaurant, their meeting was brief. I had told my dad about the incident earlier that week, and as I watched these two immigrants from a distance—one from Italy, one from Poland—shake hands, I knew that I was being cared for and loved.

That was the first and last time my father "ate" at La Croce Via. Although we never discussed it, I would bet my last dollar that my dad left work early that night so he could go to the restaurant that evening and thank Joe for the lesson he took the time to teach me.

THE DESK DRUMS

(or How Bad Things Go Good)

*"There is nothing in a caterpillar that tells
you it's going to be a butterfly."*

—Buckminster Fuller

MOST OF US ARE USUALLY QUICK to label events in our lives as "good" or "bad." In fact, although we are accustomed to defining events in this way, events themselves have no meaning other than the meaning we give them, and even then, we often can't truly know if the event is "good" or "bad" for quite some time.

I had important lessons and teachers all throughout my life, but I was surprised to have one very important teacher who was no older than I was. I was eleven years old and had just finished my first year of junior high school. I was in a two-year SP (special placement) enrichment program for "gifted" children, in which I would skip eighth grade and go directly from seventh to ninth. Most of my friends were in this class, which made me happy, and although I didn't pay too much attention to school, I was proud to always be in the most gifted classes. I sometimes wonder what my life would have been like if I'd ever applied myself. I never studied. And I always resented the kids who *said* they didn't study, but actually studied for like ten hours. When *I* said I didn't study, it meant I spent the week going to basketball practice, watching *Lost in Space*, doing the absolute minimum amount of homework needed to skate by, and then sneaking back into my sisters' room after my parents went to sleep to watch Johnny Carson.

Since I'd already skipped third grade, my skipping another grade by being in the two-year SP was a bit controversial, but, hey, that was *their* plan. I would go directly to ninth grade. Unfortunately, things weren't playing out as planned. As a "punishment" for my "disastrous" classroom behavior in seventh grade, I was being "kicked out" of the two-year SP enrichment program and was being placed in the three-year SP enrichment program, so I would have to attend eighth grade after all.

I'd always had discipline problems in school. My report cards would typically feature Ds in conduct. A C-minus grade would be accompanied by a comment such as, "Jack is improving, but he continues to bang on the desk!"

Let me tell you, I absolutely *loved* banging on the desk (aka, playing the "desk drums"), and I was good at it, too. I could play the drum solo from "Wipeout" with just one hand on the top side of a good-sounding desk! Honestly, I just couldn't stop. Truthfully, I wasn't a *bad* kid. I was just a bit unruly, and I didn't buy into the whole "blind obedience to authority" thing. Everything I'd ever heard about "just following orders" was probably already associated with Nazis. (What scares and concerns me now is that if it were today, I undoubtedly would have been diagnosed with some sort of attention deficit or hyperactivity disorder and would have been put on mood-altering medications—especially considering the banging-on-the-desk thing.) The three-year SP program was for gifted children whose parents were against the concept of skipping grades. I never bought into that. I figured these kids just weren't as smart as the two-year kids, but it looked like I'd be joining their ranks. My placement in the eighth grade was only a trial, though, and if I behaved for the first few weeks of school, I'd be transferred back to my rightful place in ninth grade with the rest of my class. I think this was meant to frighten me into submission, but this scare tactic didn't bother me much. I was pretty sure I could behave for a couple of weeks and convince everyone that I was a "good boy" who really did belong in ninth grade. I was pretty adept at working the system (like if I wanted to cut a class I'd make sure to act sick in the class before so that teacher would corroborate my story).

Enter the New York City school strike of 1968. We certainly had fun that year; it seemed like school would never start. Several months later, when school actually did go into session, my fate was sealed. It was too late for any transfers to take place. Eighth grade it was—swimming pools, movie stars . . . so much for working the system.

Being in eighth grade meant I'd have to make new friends, and I'd be faced with new teachers and new challenges. As it turns out, this particular group of gifted kids in my new grade was a pretty wild bunch. Between classes, all of the really big kids (of whom I was one) would "run interference." This consisted of running through the hallways as fast as possible and knocking down any students who happened to be in the way. *Nice.* Then there was the time they dangled poor Freddie out of the second-floor window by his legs. Perhaps they should have left me in the two-year SP program with the "smart," wimpy kids.

Of course, having an extra year in school did give us time for additional enrichments, including instrumental music. Other than my desk, I had never played a musical instrument in my life. As luck would have it, I was blessed by two converging forces: one was Steve Feldman and the other was Michael Willner.

Steve Feldman was the music teacher at Meyer Levin Junior High School. He was a saxophone player with a club-date business on the side called Steve Fields Orchestra. His band played at private events such as weddings, bar mitzvahs, and dinner dances. He was a good guy and seemed to truly care about teaching the kids, although I'm guessing he probably would have preferred to just be a player. He was an open-minded and flexible teacher, which proved life-altering for me.

Michael Willner was the most unusual student I'd ever met. He was of medium build and appearance, with a short, always neat hairdo of side-combed, sandy-brown hair. He wore heavy-rimmed spectacles and always sported a shirt and tie—sometimes a bowtie. He was absolutely the smartest kid in the entire school, and he had impeccable behavior. Any attempt to address him during class would result in a raised hand, palm out, in a clear signal that you immediately refrain from any further efforts at communication while class was in session. Michael was also an incredible percussionist, and that was the root of our unlikely friendship.

On that first day in class, when Mr. Feldman asked what instrument I wanted to play, I made the obvious choice: drums. I guess it was *bashert* (meant to be) that I would be a drummer one way or the other.

Mr. Feldman had a dilemma of sorts when it came to me. I was at least a year and a half behind everyone in my class at playing an instrument. Michael Willner, on the other hand, was far ahead of the class. Mr. Feldman creatively arranged for the two of us to spend class time in the cafeteria, where Michael would bring me up to date. This is where I appreciated Mr. Feldman's flexibility and desire to have kids really learn. Another teacher might have just had me catch up slowly in the classroom.

Michael and I spent many an afternoon in that cafeteria under the stark glow of fluorescent lights. We chose an area in one of the seemingly endless rows of long rectangular tables to set up our drum pads, and we spent hours playing paradiddles, flams, and ratamacues. Michael was stiff but kind. He was just a boy himself, but he had fantastic discipline. Many other kids would have just goofed off the entire period, but Michael treated our sessions like class time. And he was talented. He was in the all-city band, and his rudiments were as clean as any I've ever heard. He was the perfect teacher, and I knew I was fortunate to have him.

As it became clear that I also had some aptitude, we developed a friendship of sorts. We didn't really socialize together after school, although I went to his house once or twice. I was with the "in" crowd, and he was the school egghead. It was more that we had an unspoken understanding—a kind of secret two-person society of our own making. It was a complex relationship, one of teacher and student, of peers, and of friendship.

The day finally came when Michael informed me that I had caught up to the curriculum, and we should be returning to the classroom. I had come to dread the prospect of this day. I knew how much more he had to offer, and by now, I was totally hooked on playing the drums.

I begged him not to tell Mr. Feldman. I suggested we continue our sessions so he could continue to teach me whatever he could. I knew this would be an extremely difficult decision for Michael, and I was banking on the friendship we had created to lean him toward my way of thinking. He was accustomed to following the rules, yet now he would have to actively mislead a teacher. I could feel how much it took for him, but he somehow summoned the courage and agreed, for which I will always be grateful. Our meetings would continue.

By the time we finally returned to class instruction, I was so far ahead of everyone else in the percussion section (except Michael, of course) that Mr. Feldman agreed to let me learn another instrument during class time, as long as I played percussion when needed and for concerts. I played trumpet, French horn, mellophone, Eb horn, and something I think was called horn in F. A whole new world opened up to me, and it wasn't just musical. This was the first time, aside from playing sports, when I really felt like trying my best. I confirmed everyone's suspicion that I had musical talent, but to my surprise, I found that I was also willing to work hard at it.

When our days in the cafeteria ended, the special friendship between Michael and me also waned, but it never entirely disappeared. We always knew that we had shared something very special and unique.

I soon began studying privately with one of Mr. Feldman's regular drummers and would often carry his drums to gigs on the weekends. Mr. Feldman would give me a chance to "sit in" and play on one or two tunes during the evening. It didn't take long before I was working with the Steve Fields Orchestra for real and getting paid, too. (My dad could never quite believe anyone would actually pay me for the

banging he heard when I practiced at home.) Playing the drums made me feel free. I could lose myself in it, even when I was just practicing alone—I still can. I loved it from the start, which is probably why I felt so bad when my dad once asked me if I didn't want to play a "real" instrument. I think he felt pretty awful when he saw the look on my face, too. But I know what my dad meant: Drums don't feature melody or harmony in the same way that, say, a piano does, but drums feature balance, power, and subtlety as well. And when you've got every limb moving independently to the groove (and also singing), the feeling is indescribable (and chicks dig it, too).

With the Steve Fields Orchestra, I learned to play drum beats for the rhumba, bossa nova, mambo, waltz, cha-cha, fox-trot, and merengue, and sang songs like "Aquarius" and "Let the Sunshine In." I loved singing, too, and I was getting great experience. Soon, I began getting gigs with other bands and going up to the Catskill Mountains to play in hotel bands for the summer. I continued to learn more and more about music, and I ultimately went on to become a successful drummer and later a singer and entertainer. It would seem that the "punishment" for misbehaving in seventh grade changed my life forever—as it turns out, for the better.

This is obviously a story of childhood, but its theme and message far transcend childhood. Events that seem "bad" at the time can often turn out to be "good" in the long run. This event taught me that it's always wise to withhold judgment about whether a thing is "good" or "bad." Of course, that can be difficult. Yet, sometimes, the most challenging circumstances create new opportunities we might not have otherwise had. Keeping an open and flexible mind and staying vigilant in the pursuit of silver linings are important keys to success.

Although I probably did not have these notions as a boy, I was nonetheless able to make the most of a seemingly "bad" event. I see it clearly now. Oftentimes, circumstances that shake us up and break our sometimes passive routines force us to find our own inner strength and personal power. Because they free us from the "known" in our lives and lead us into the unknown, they can unleash untapped reservoirs of passion and creativity. I have learned that unplanned or even unwelcome events can make us focus on what is real and important to us—like when a family loses their house in a tornado but ends up realizing that it was only stuff or even when someone loses a loved one and it spurs them to pursue medicine, pass legislation, or reform their lives.

It's a theme I come back to often—while some events are outside of our control, we alone get to define *what those events mean to us* and how we use them. We alone get to decide whether they are a beginning or an end.

So, this is usually about the time in the discussion when my son wants to start rolling his eyes up into his head. He's a good kid, so he resists the temptation, but I can just imagine his internal dialogue: "Daddy, I get it—you messed up in school, you learned to play the drums, great! Does *everything* have to be a lesson?"

DAD

(or "Be Like Your Father")

"We know what a person thinks not when he tells us what he thinks, but by his actions."

—Isaac Bashevis Singer

ACTIONS SPEAK LOUDER THAN WORDS. *Do as I say, not as I do.* These are just a couple of the sayings that convey the age-old message that it is our behavior, not our words, that reflects who we are, what we believe, and how we will ultimately be judged. Children learn by watching their parents, and I am no exception. Although my dad and I talked extensively—especially later in life—much of what I learned from him came from observing his behavior throughout the years, and later, after he died, learning about his benevolence from people who had known him.

My dad was a wise, yet simple man, and a straight shooter. He was an extremely principled man, and ethics always determined his course of action. He worked very hard—never drank, smoked, or philandered. Spending money at restaurants or on movies was a rare extravagance for him. Yes, he was a frugal man. But don't mistake *frugal* for *cheap*. There is an important difference, as I learned throughout my life by observing him.

My dad also had a great love for planting and watching things grow. His garden was always his refuge from the troubles of his world. When he became disillusioned with the traditional notion of God after the Holocaust, my father regained his faith through the wonder and miracle of growing things. In his retirement years, he would begin gardening at dawn and not finish until dark. Instead of using pesticides, he would carefully remove bugs from the leaves and stems by hand, and he would always leave some of his crop unprotected for the local birds and other animals.

He also took great pride in giving the fruits of his labors to his friends and neighbors. When I moved into the area where my dad lived and was setting up my utility account, the operator at the utility company asked if I was related to the guy who always paid his bill in person along with a bag of organic tomatoes. I laughed, and I was proud to say that I was indeed his son.

My dad was a hugely literate person who spoke six languages and mixed his passions for social justice, Yiddish culture, and gardening together in his own large volume of published writings. In fact, when he died, I inherited his vast personal library of Yiddish and English books. Just by looking at the diverse array of titles, I got to know him better.

It had always been my dad's dream to live in the mountains, which is very much in line with the organic gardener he was at heart, but when he arrived in the United States, he was told that his family would starve if they didn't live in the city, which is why we lived in Manhattan and eventually ended up in Brooklyn. The truth is my father would have done fine anywhere. When he retired, he finally took up residence in Kiamesha Lake, New York, in the heart of the Catskill Mountains.

I was in my midtwenties when my dad asked me to come for a visit to the mountains to discuss his last will and testament. At the time, we were at odds over how I approached my finances. In stark contrast to my dad's dedication to saving a portion of his paycheck even when he made as little as thirty dollars a week, I quickly spent whatever money I earned. He'd complain that I had "no respect for the dollar." And I'd retort with, "A dollar is just a piece of paper. It has no inherent value of its own like hard work or honesty. Why should it earn my respect?"

Of course, I knew the point he was trying to make, but I enjoyed being difficult at that age. I used to tell him that I had trouble with money because I was genetically designed to be a philanthropist and my DNA was confused, given our family history (our family had been wealthy before the war). If not for the Holocaust, I would be running foundations to save the world. He would just say, "Not everything is a joke." In any event, despite the many disagreements we had concerning how I handled money, I was his son, and of course I would be there to support him during these discussions.

On this occasion, we met with a local attorney who had been referred by a friend. We were in the attorney's office discussing the will, when the lawyer suggested to me that I should give my dad and him some privacy.

"Why do we need privacy?" my father asked, in a voice that betrayed some surprise.

The attorney responded that it was for his protection.

"What kind of protection?" my dad asked.

"Protection of your assets during your lifetime," the lawyer responded.

"From who?" asked my dad.

"Well, from your son," the attorney responded, shifting uncomfortably in his chair.

I'm sure my long hair, unshaven face, and general rock-'n'-roll look couldn't have inspired much confidence—but, to be honest, I think he might have said the same even if I looked like an Ivy League alumni. I didn't hold it against him; he didn't know us.

My father leaned forward and spoke slowly and deliberately. "Sir," he began, "I appreciate you are just doing what you think is in my best interest. But if I have to worry about my son defrauding me then he might as well have it all right now, because my life would be over anyway."

My dad's response didn't surprise me. I knew he'd do anything for me. Still, what he said made me proud, because it so clearly laid out the priorities in his life. It also publicly displayed his trust and unconditional love for me, despite his private disapproval of my approach to money.

I learned a lot about my dad in lawyers' offices, on that occasion and others. For example, when my mother became ill with early-onset Alzheimer's disease, we searched out an elder rights attorney with regard to the enormous cost of her care. She had needed private-pay home care for a very long time, and then had to be moved to an actual nursing facility. Those costs would be even more enormous and impossible for us to pay. Getting government assistance through the Medicare program would require my father to spend his remaining savings down to almost nothing.

The attorney said there was an easy solution to the problem. My dad could simply divorce my mother, and his obligation to pay would be ended. The state would then pick up the tab for her care.

My father refused.

The attorney patiently explained that this wasn't a real divorce in the traditional sense. Of course my father would still care for and love my mother. It would simply prevent him from having to spend himself into poverty to insure her care. He was sure my mom wouldn't want him to do that. This was a financial decision, not an emotional one.

"No," my father said. He simply wouldn't do it. I know he understood it was just a formality, but it was one he couldn't live with. My father had promised my mother's family that he would take care of her when they left Poland, and he would fulfill that promise.

The attorney gave me a beseeching look, but I was too proud of my father to be of much use. It was amazing to see a person stand on principle that way. In any case, I already knew that my father had remained married to my mother all of these years because of that promise. I was not surprised by his refusal to divorce her now when she most needed to be cared for.

Ultimately, my father and the government entered into an arrangement to split the cost of my mother's nursing-home care, but it was still a large financial burden. Nevertheless, he cared for her in this way for the rest of her natural life.

On an earlier occasion at an attorney's office, I delightfully witnessed the dissolution of my father's thirty-year-long partnership with Aaron Katz upon my dad's retirement from the business. There were four of us in the office. My father, Aaron, the attorney, and me.

As my father and Aaron were talking, the attorney turned to me and said quietly, "Watch this carefully, because this sort of thing doesn't happen anymore. Their entire business relationship has been based on a handshake many years ago. I'm here only as a formality to sign off on whatever they work out. What you're witnessing is something from a time gone by. The last of an era."

I was fairly taken aback by this. I began listening closely to their conversation. As they divvied up the assets, I felt like I was watching an old Abbott and Costello routine.

"Wait a minute, remember when your cousin came to visit, you gave him that maroon three-piece crushed velvet sectional sofa?" one would recall.

"Yeah, and, what about when your wife was sick, you took money to pay that *fakakte* doctor!" replied the other.

Sure enough, they worked it all out in good humor. Aaron was never happy that my father left the business, but my dad had worked all his life (as did Aaron), and he simply had his hands full with my mother and her disease.

I have always been fond of the story about how my dad and Aaron wound up owning a block of ten stores. The block of buildings where their store was located was going to be sold. Their lease was up, and the new prospective owner wanted their store for his own use. Their only chance to keep their store was to buy the building themselves, but there was a problem since they didn't have the money. They contacted all of their suppliers and explained the situation. They asked for loans and also a moratorium on payments for supplies for a period of time, until they could get on their feet. The suppliers agreed. Aaron and my dad purchased the building, changing their lives forever. Something like this could only be accomplished by people with impeccable reputations, and it taught me that reputation is everything. In both his business and personal life, my father operated with genuine honesty, and everyone he dealt with could be assured of that. I recall a story from my bar mitzvah celebration that is emblazoned in my memory. A few of my father's business associates, suppliers, and even competitors had been invited, and several of them surrounded me at some point during the party and spoke to me quite earnestly: "Be like your father," they implored me. "Your father is an honest man. Be like your father."

Their words made quite an impression on me as a young boy. I knew my dad was different from most, and I was proud of his work ethic and what he'd accomplished, but he seemed straightlaced and boring—not exciting or cool. Hearing men talk about his honesty and witnessing the value they attributed to it reminded me of how unusual my father was. I'll never forget that feeling of pride.

One last story about my dad amply illustrates the difference between my father's words and deeds. I took care of a rental property we had for a few years as my dad got older. In one of the apartments, a married couple began to get seriously behind on their rent. They'd just had a child with some health issues, so I was patient. They got further and further behind. Each time I approached them about it, the man told me he was doing his best, and he would definitely be paying the rent soon. I told him to keep me abreast of what was happening. He assured me he'd be fine soon. However, they got even further behind, but I didn't have the heart to press them, considering the kid. They were eight or nine months in arrears when they skipped out during the night.

When I told my dad what had happened, he just smiled. He said he loved me and I was a nice guy, but I was a putz who shouldn't be in business. He had seen this coming a mile away. I felt a bit embarrassed, but we took it as a loss and that was that.

Then, about two years ago, just after my father's death, I was going through my dad's papers when I found a stack of letters from the pastor of the Whole Truth Church, which was on the site of my dad's first store. The church had purchased the building from my dad and Aaron, and they held a mortgage for the church. According to the documents, the church hit some hard times and couldn't make the mortgage payments. The letters were personal thank-you notes addressed to my dad for allowing them to continue in the building without payment. There were many, many letters as they fell further and further behind. The pastor thanked him over and over for his patience and kindness and understanding. He blessed him and prayed that God would send blessings to him and his family and said that the congregation prayed for him at the church.

My dad may have ridiculed me for being too easy on tenants, but my father's actions always spoke louder than his words ever could.

My father was a wise and humble man who lived a quiet life. Except when he marched for social justice, fought against inequality, or wrote the truth when it wasn't convenient or popular, or spoke fearlessly on behalf of the disenfranchised. He waged a courageous battle with Parkinson's disease and took pride that he kept his wits about him, even near the end.

About a week before he passed, my producing partners told me they'd like to meet him; we all knew the end was near. I explained to my dad in Yiddish that my *shitifs* (partners) were going to come visit him. He could barely speak any longer, but he tried to whisper something. I felt awful, but I had to ask him to repeat it several times before I could make it out. He was saying *shutvim*, which is the correct Yiddish word for partners. My dad was still teaching me up until the very end.

A few weeks earlier, I had arbitrarily turned to my dad one afternoon and said, "Hey, Pop, you know you've been the most important influence in my life, right?"

He nodded that he did. I knew he did, but I wanted to make sure I said it out loud.

On the occasion of my dad's first birthday after his death, I told my son, Dovy, that surprisingly I wasn't sad. I explained that I wasn't sad because his *zeyde* (grandpa) was well prepared and unafraid to die; he was at home, surrounded by loved ones, and it was his time—but also because my father and I had told each other everything we needed to while he was alive. There was no unfinished business to feel bad about.

There are so many lessons I learned by watching my dad, probably too many to enumerate. The courage and dignity he showed in the last few years of his life were a lesson to us all. And at my show, I hear so many wonderful stories from so many people who somehow knew my father. At times it almost seems as though, through the way he  lived his life, he continues to teach me and my son, even from beyond the grave.

Ultimately, the most powerful lessons I learned from my father are as simple and timeless as he was. Live your ideals, never compromise your integrity, and let your actions speak for who you are.

MOM

(or Remembering the Comfort of Her Care)

"Youth fades; love droops; the leaves of friendship fall;
a mother's secret hope outlives them all."

—Washington Irving

THE EARLIEST, AND PERHAPS MOST IMPORTANT, influence in our lives is our parents. In the early years, they are our main mirror for self-referral, and they set the earliest foundation for how we view the world and our surroundings. They provide us (consciously or not) with the first tools we will use to interpret our journey through life. It often takes well into adulthood (if ever) for people

to fully understand and make peace with their parental relationship, and it tends to color all others. While it is true that each of us comes into the world with our own spirit and intention, in most cases our parents exert the most profound external influence on our lives.

In my family, my father's influence and approval was paramount—in my life and in our household. Though he was at work much of the time, his expectations were the driving force behind everything we did. For generations, the Ehrenreich family has been a powerful and passionate force (the actual translation of the name is "rich in honor"), and that energy continues on today with my son, Dovy. My wife, Lisa, says he's always been "daddy's boy," but I say he is simply following in the Ehrenreich tradition.

My mother's influence on me was more subtle, even though she was the parent who was most around when I was growing up. Over the years, I've come to more fully recognize those parts of me that reflect her influence, and not surprisingly, these are the softer, more ethereal, less intellectual aspects of my persona. I don't know that I ever got to thank my mother for these gifts in her lifetime, and I'm not even sure I was fully aware of their effect on me when she was alive. Although I showed my love for her in many ways, and even more often as I got older, she needed and would have welcomed much more—from all of us.

When I was very young, my mom would sing me to sleep with three lullabies—one in Russian, one in Polish, and one in Yiddish—and then pat my back until I fell asleep. Amazingly, I remembered all three lullabies into adulthood, and it was one of my mom's great joys that I did—and mine, too. She often asked me to sing them to her, and we laughed. As my mom's early-onset Alzheimer's disease progressed, she'd ask me to sing them to her more frequently, and ultimately the songs became one of the few things that seemed to bring her peace. Even in the last years—when it was clear she no longer recognized me—I would sing them to her again in the hopes that my voice, the words, and the melody would somehow enter her consciousness.

My mom's parenting style was natural and instinctive. One afternoon I came home from playing with an umbrella handle stuck in my mouth. She didn't hesitate to yank it out, along with half the flesh on my inner cheeks. When my sister Joanie went to the emergency room with knitting needles stuck in her throat (don't ask) and the doctor demurred from removing them, my mother dove right in and pulled them out. We always knew we could count on her in a pinch. (So to speak.)

Unfortunately, my mother was never really 100-percent emotionally "stable." We used to say she never got a chance to grow up, because of the war. Even as a young boy, I understood that about her. She had been ravaged by the deaths of her family in the Holocaust and was a victim of a different sort.

My mom was only sixteen when she left German-occupied Poland with my father and a small group of others, for what was to be a short while until things calmed down. Young Jewish men were starting to be taken away under Nazi occupation; my dad was nineteen, and he had just illegally reburied a boy in a Jewish cemetery who had been shot and killed by the Nazis. My parents were headed to a sort of no-man's land between Russian-occupied Poland and German-occupied Poland. My father was a well-respected young man and the leader of a local youth group. He and my mom were dating at the time, and he gave her family his word that if she went with them, he would take care of her until they could return. They never could. My father lived his whole life carrying out that promise. For my mother's part, I don't believe she would have left with him had she known she would never see her family again.

Shortly after my folks left their hometown, Germany attacked Russia, and my parents were eventually sent to work camps in Siberia, deep inside Russia. My mother always held out hope of seeing her family again, and she cried herself to sleep every night. She and my dad made three aborted attempts to escape back to Poland. Had they been successful, they probably would not be alive today.

Every Friday night during my childhood, when my mother lit the Shabbos candles, she would cry. I have vivid images in my head of seeing her in the dining room, her head covered in a white lace *tikhel*, as she passed her arms over the candles and said the prayers. It now seems odd and sad that we left her alone during that time, but I guess none of us really wanted to deal with her emotional connection to the past too much. My father never spoke of the past at all while I was a child. I can't understand how we didn't find a way to just walk over and be with her.

When I was in elementary school, I'd often come home to find my mom sitting at our little kitchen table, her eyes red from all the tears. She'd smile when she saw me and call me over in Yiddish, "Yankele, kim shoyn, zetz zikh anider, lomir redn." (My sweet Yankele, come already, sit down, let's talk.)

Reluctantly, I'd take a seat across from her. She would tell me about the family she still missed so much, and again she would cry. The story of her brother Joseph sticks in my mind. He survived the war but perished when the ship he was on, which was bound for freedom in America, was mistakenly bombed by allied forces at the end of the war. It was uncomfortable and confusing for me to see my mom cry like that and to hear her stories. I didn't know what to do with the emotion—hers or mine—or how to comfort her. I realize now I could have just listened. I was just a young boy, but I've always felt a bit guilty about not being there more for my mom. I would sit for a while, but I was really more interested in going out and playing with my friends.

Amazingly, my mom was joyful and friendly and outgoing. Her speech was a cross between English and Yiddish. With a naturally upbeat, outward personality, she was well liked by the neighborhood store owners. Her quirky and slightly confused behavior was actually endearing. Whenever someone asked her age, she would go ahead and tell them, then say, "But I don't look it." I admired how she was quick to compliment herself and didn't bother waiting to hear it from someone else. (That's creating your own reality, all right.)

But I could tell that my mom was very lonely, and the few distant friends she had were extremely important to her. I felt as if I needed to care for her, but that was hard for me to admit and actually carry out. She would sometimes ask me to sit and play cards with her in the middle of the afternoon, and although I felt sorry for her, I was busy trying to live my American life and fit in—and my mom wasn't helping. But I occasionally broke down and played with her, and even enjoyed learning and playing a rummy game called Kalookie.

The lack of a good loving relationship with my father certainly increased my mom's isolation and loneliness. And the fights they had would sometimes send me and my sisters huddling together in the back room.

My father worked all the time and in those days was not a very social person. He was more of an intellectual type, and my mother was the type who enjoyed dancing and going out to have a good time—not that she often got the chance. My dad almost never took her out. One of the few times he did take her out resulted in one of those quirky family dysfunctional stories we later came to tell and retell. It always seemed that our humorous family stories had some sadness in them—which fits in so well with the story of our people— "laughter though the tears," they say.

My dad was taking my mom to a show (with us kids in tow, of course) at one of the Yiddish theaters in Manhattan, and he got stopped for a traffic infraction. We were running late as it was, and my mother laid into the poor cop as he approached the car window.

"Mister, he never takes me anywhere! Never! The one time he takes me out, you stop him for a ticket? We're going to be late if you keep us here, and he never takes me anywhere!"

She went on and on for a while, and the force of her indignation finally convinced the police officer to let us go. I guess he just figured my dad had enough on his plate without his adding to it, and dealing with my outraged immigrant mother was more than he had bargained for. He had his own problems.

One of our other funny but sad recurring stories happened every Passover. We would prepare a traditional Passover Seder, and my dad would lead it. The Seder service includes drinking four glasses of red wine during the evening. We never made it past the first glass.

Soon after drinking the first glass of wine, my mom's face would get very red and flushed. Shortly thereafter, we would begin to see the beginnings of laughter. She would look at my sisters and me with the most serious face she could muster, but we knew it was just a bluff. Soon her head was down on the table, and you could visibly see her shaking from laughter. She never drank, and it turned out she was allergic to red wine and just couldn't help herself. It was great to see my mom really laugh like that, and my sisters and I would promptly start to laugh as well (much to my father's dismay).

When I attended college on Long Island, I would often hitchhike back to Brooklyn. This really upset my mom, and she made me promise not to hitch*kike*. As in many cases, she just mispronounced the word. I'd say, "Ma, I promise not to hitch*kike*"—then I would go hitch*hike* back to school. Come to think of it, maybe "hitch*kike*" is just a word for Jewish hitchhiking. (All right, take it easy. Now every *Yenta* is going to call the Anti-Defamation League.)

As odd as this may sound, some of my fondest memories of my mother are from when I was sick. I'd moan for her from my bedroom ("Maaaaaaaaa!"), and when she would come, I'd pathetically say, "Mom, I'm dying." I'd do this repeatedly, a dozen times or more— my moans becoming longer, louder, and higher pitched—until I finally got her to laugh. Although she protested, this was one of our great joys together. God bless my mother. She loved me so much she had to see if I was okay, even though she knew I was fooling around. (By the way, moaning nice and loud when you're sick really does make you feel better. Try it some time. I now do it with my wife when I'm not feeling well, although, she'll only come in once or twice to see if I'm okay, so it's not as much fun.)

Since my mom was always a bit confused, it was hard to recognize the early signs of Alzheimer's disease. At the time, little was known about the condition (much less early-onset Alzheimer's disease), and people simply called it senility. My mother was too young to be going senile, but it was hard to deny there was a problem. My dad started to complain that my mother was doing spiteful things, such as tossing a slab of meat on a plate for dinner and not cooking any vegetables to go with it. So I decided to take a drive over to my parents' new home in Upstate New York to see what was up.

It was during that visit when I realized something was very wrong. My mother smelled like urine, and it appeared that she hadn't changed her clothes in a while. If nothing else, she'd always been super clean.

"Ma, is everything alright?" I asked. "Your clothes look a little funny."

I was really concerned, but she refused to talk about it. I took my dad aside and wondered if he had noticed that Mom smelled bad. He didn't, which was not that surprising, since my father was no basket of potpourri himself. He ate tons of raw garlic every day and, in those days, generally practiced personal hygiene reminiscent of a fifteenth-century pirate.

I tried to convince him that this wasn't just spiteful behavior and thought my mom might be clinically depressed. I believed the isolation of living in the country couldn't be helping my mother, so I suggested they move closer to us and to the city immediately. I thought more time spent with me and my sisters and the additional emotional support that it would bring would help her. My father agreed to move closer. We arbitrarily picked a town half way back to New York City, where my father could still have his garden, but by the time we found a home for my parents to move into, my mother's disease had progressed so far that she needed to be moved into a nursing facility to be properly cared for. She lived her last years at the Workmen's Circle Home for the Aged in the Bronx. Ultimately, my mom wound up in a fetal position and finally passed in 1989 at age sixty-seven.

I don't know what my mother would have been like if the

Holocaust hadn't taken its evil toll on the world and on her personally. Perhaps she would have developed normally or perhaps she just had a weak disposition. I'm disposed to believe that the warm and loving qualities she exhibited in her life would have made her turn out just fine. In general, I know the upheaval she experienced at an early age, and later the stress and loneliness, and the lack of the love she needed definitely affected the way her life turned out. The same would later be true of my sisters, Joanie and Wanda. At least my mom had us.

I loved my mother dearly and hold many wonderful memories of her in my heart. She could be immature and needy, but she could also be joyful, funny, loving, and generous—and she was devoted to me. She was my mother, and I was her "Yankele," and she loved and cared for me always.

Many years ago, when I was on one of my first road gigs in Pennsylvania, I got the flu. I somehow packed myself into my car and drove to my parent's house in Brooklyn. My mom put me to bed, made a big pot of chicken soup, and nursed me back to health.

There is no place in the world that could have felt as safe and comforting as being home with my mom. She soothed me and waited on me hand and foot, and when I moaned, "Maaaaaaaaa!" she was there, as she had always been.

THE CATSKILLS
(or What Was, Was, and Is No More)

*"To look backward for a while is to refresh the eye,
to restore it, and to render it more fit for its
prime function of looking forward."*

—Margaret Fairless Barber

I'VE ALWAYS BEEN FASCINATED by what happens when things that seem permanent go away—like vinyl records or abandoned castles or unused rail lines. They always carry something sad about them, and in the case of places, they seem to retain an emotional feeling—almost an echo, or a remnant, of their former glory that can still be sensed. One of the truly important and formative places in my life, both personally and professionally, has come to have that air about it.

The breathtaking Catskill Mountains in Upstate New York played a monumental role in all aspects of my life. Featured in movies like *Dirty Dancing* and *A Walk on the Moon*, the Borscht Belt (as this part of the Catskill Mountain range was often referred to) was a lush, mountainous resort area about 100 miles north of New York City. The area was home to some of the world's most famous hotels and dozens of smaller hotels and bungalow colonies. In its heyday of the fifties and sixties, the Catskills featured such performers as

Jerry Lewis, Eddie Fisher, and Sammy Davis Jr., as well as sports stars like Rocky Graziano and later Wilt Chamberlain and Oscar Robertson. Many famous entertainers got their start in the Catskills, including Sid Caesar, Danny Kaye, Mel Brooks, and many, many others.

But there was another Catskills that was very important to me and to my family: the bungalow colonies where we spent every summer when I was a kid. My family was never wealthy enough to afford hotels, but the smaller bungalow colonies were within our reach.

Near the end of the school year, the anticipation of going to the mountains would start to build. The summer seemed like an eternity then, and I looked forward to the experiences of a whole lifetime away from the city. On July Fourth weekend, we'd load up our car, tie a few old lawn chairs from the garage on top, and head up to our bungalow in the Catskills. The sense of joy and excitement began in the car on the ride up. In the old days, we traveled old Route 17, a single-lane highway that was the only way upstate, along with about a billion other cars. It was like the exodus of Moses leading the Jews out of Egypt except with a stop at the Red Apple Rest, where everyone went to pee. This was the signal that we were halfway to paradise. After being surrounded by brick and concrete all year long, the idea of playing in the grass, going swimming and boating, seeing my summer "cousins," and being next to nature was the most exciting thing imaginable.

When we first started going, we stayed at a very small place called Roshvalbs in Greenfield Park, near Ellenville. I was just an infant, but I still have the fifty-dollar U.S. savings bond my father bought for me that first summer of 1957. Roshvalbs was a *kokhaleyn*, which in

Yiddish literally means "cook alone" or "cook by yourself." It was a small cluster of old summer shacks and a main house with rooms for rent. The recreation was swimming in the nearby creek where we used tire inner tubes as floats. We were new immigrants with very little money, but my father always said that those were the best times of our lives.

Later, we graduated to full-fledged bungalow colonies, which carried names like the White House Bungalows or Paradise Estates. A bungalow colony was still just a bunch of non-air-conditioned shacks, but they weren't shy about their names. The names of these places reflected what they represented, not the décor of the buildings. These "fancier" bungalow colonies featured a swimming pool, a concession where you could buy lunch, and eventually even a "casino" with entertainment on Saturday nights. I'm not sure why they called these places casinos, since there was certainly no gambling. The only gambling occurred at the concession where you took your chances when ordering a hamburger for lunch.

Years later when I was dating Miss North Carolina, I made the mistake of telling her my family rented a bungalow for the summer. She perked up. I could tell she was picturing something out of *The Great Gatsby*. I tried to calm her excitement by explaining these bungalows were in Monticello. That only made things worse—she thought I was referring to Thomas Jefferson's historic estate. I made a mental note to stop mentioning bungalow colonies to my non-Jewish girlfriends.

We always went to the bungalow colonies with other immigrant families (*green-eh* families, which is Yiddish for "greenhorn"). Each family rented a bungalow for the entire summer. Like my family, the moms and kids stayed all season, and the men worked in the city during the week and came up on the weekends they could get away. Bungalow colonies were the perfect place for all types of families with children. They were an

escape from the hot, noisy city where the kids would be safe and occupied, and the parents could enjoy some genuine "off" time. But this was especially true for our Holocaust-survivor families.

Here was a place where our parents were able to relax together with people like themselves and really let their guards down. They played cards, spoke in Yiddish or Polish, and even hit a soccer ball or two. It was a special treat to see my parents as well as my friends' parents, who had had so much tragedy in their lives, forget their troubles and just enjoy themselves. Sometimes, it seemed as if they hadn't a care in the world, and that made us feel better, too. For short periods during those fabulous youthful summers, it almost seemed as if we could just be normal.

We always rented bungalows together in a cluster. At Ryke Inn Colony in Kiamesha Lake—where I have most of my memories—we rented up on the hill. Up the hill was our own little world where I personally felt most like everyone else. This was a place where the residents could roll up their sleeves and if they had a number on their arm, nobody looked twice. We were more like family than friends; in fact, we often referred to each other as cousins and relatives to fill in for those lost in the *milkhome* (the war).

All the parents on the hill had heavy accents and names like Shmulek and Mendel, which made Yonkee seem as American as if I'd arrived on the Mayflower. My best friend's name was "Keevy." I think if someone had shouted "John" or "Mary" at the top of their lungs, one of us probably would have called the cops.

We kids played outside all day long, catching frogs and playing baseball, dodge ball, basketball, Ping Pong, volleyball—every outdoor game imaginable. Of course we played with the "American" kids, too, and we were all considered equal. But when we went in for the night, it was back up the hill to our little self-imposed *shtetl* (town). Despite feeling very much a part of survivor-based Jewish life in the Catskills, we were still outsiders. I envied those kids with regular American parents and regular American lives who stayed down the hill. I didn't yet understand that they had their own sets of problems, too.

I used to take hikes with my dad, and we'd pick berries or even go boating. When we went boating, though, he made us stay close to shore because he couldn't swim. I used to love the outfit he wore—a white tank top with lime-green bathing trunks, which partially covered two spindly legs, and a pair of shiny black dress shoes and socks.

I learned to swim early on, but I was the only one in my family who ever did. If I ate anything at all, even a crumb, my mom wouldn't let me go in the water for at least an hour. She said I'd get a cramp and drown. I would always shave a few minutes off the time and then have terrible guilt thinking what would happen if I drowned after all.

When we got a little older, many of us went to day camp at another bungalow colony just up the road. The grandfather from the family-owned Lakeside Villa (bungalow colonies were almost always family owned and operated) would make numerous trips back and forth in his station wagon to bring us kids to camp. We must have had thirty kids each trip—we rode on the roof, hanging off the back, and on the hood. No one ever fell off, but Jeffrey Mermelfein threw up in the backseat once. I think he just had food poisoning from the concession.

Even though I liked camp, waking up so early was a drag. To my utter horror, every morning, bright and early, the PA system at the bungalow colony would blare "Wake Up Little Suzy." It wouldn't actually wake me up, but it was a cue to my mother that it was time to rouse me from my deep, comfortable sleep.

Waking up the kids was the main use for the PA system along with notifying the whole colony anytime someone got a phone call or to announce the arrival of Ruby, the knish man. But no other announcements were ever as early or as loud as "Wake Up Little Suzy." I still know all the words to that song by heart, and I can only assume that every family in our colony had a kid in camp, because I can't recall any murders ever being reported on account of it.

One morning, my mother decided to let me sleep late. Unfortunately, she chose the day of the BIG miniature golf trip. I was so disappointed, but also conflicted. I knew my mom was trying to do something nice for me and I saw how sad my disappointment made her. It was really hard to be mad at her, but I never quite got over it. I'd probably be a rich, famous golfer today if not for that missed field trip. I ended up spending the day catching frogs down by the stream near the handball court where the handyman lived. He had one glass eye that always looked in a different direction, and you never knew for sure who he was talking to. I always wondered if that's what it was like talking to Sammy Davis Jr. up close.

My whole family seemed to thrive in the Catskills. Somehow the fresh air and the freedom of the setting made everything and everybody just seem happier—more joyful and carefree. It was a time when the nightmares of the war years were somehow put aside for another day. We were less dysfunctional there, and I will always reserve a very special place in my heart for those times and those places.

My family stopped going to bungalow colonies when I got my first gig in the Catskills as a musician. I was so young that half the summer I played drums in a band, and half the summer I went to sleepaway camp! I worked for an agent named Sammy. If you asked Sammy how much the gig paid, he would say, "Hey, there's gonna be girls there!" (And there were.)

That first gig paid thirty-five dollars per week, and in retrospect, I should have paid Sammy for the incredible training I began that summer. The Catskills were the greatest training ground in the world and there were so many hotels that they needed as many musicians as they could get. The bigger hotels could afford the more experienced professionals, but the small places could only afford kids. (Neil Sedaka was one of the "kids" who started as a bandleader at one of the small places called the Esther Manor. He married the owner's daughter!) And we really learned. It was the kind of place where, if you made a mistake, you kept your job . . . even if you made mistake after mistake, you still kept your job. There's no place like that today . . . well, maybe the Oval Office.

The Catskills had some of the world's most lavish hotels, and the finest entertainment as well—it was like the Las Vegas of the east without the gambling. The non-famous acts would often play several shows in an evening and move from the big fancy hotels for the early show, all the way down to the small hotels and bungalow colonies for the late show. Because of that system, we'd get to play with fairly good acts, even in the tiny places. Sometimes we couldn't play their music or "charts," even with a long rehearsal. Upon realizing this, the act would calmly collect the music, then ask, "Do you know *You're Nobody Till Somebody Loves You* in B flat?" They'd end up putting together a whole "fake" show on the spot.

All of this made a huge impression on me, and I learned so much from watching these performers. As time went on, I perfected my craft and got into the really great hotels with the best musicians and performers—this all stood me in good stead for the rest of my career from nightclubs to touring to Broadway, both as a musician and a performer. No matter what kind of gigs I've done, I could never replace the training I got in the Catskills.

I grew up socially in the Catskills as well. Not only with peers of my own age, but also with much older people. As I moved to the larger hotels, my bandmates tended to be adults, and I also got friendly with some of the acts.

Sometimes, this age difference thing didn't go as smoothly as one would have hoped. The bandleader/pianist at the Stevensville Hotel was Jack Kahn, a nice guy probably in his late sixties at the time. I was a young wiseass kid, but we liked each other. The bone of contention between Jack and me was that I was always late. Not *really* late, but just enough to raise his blood pressure; I would frequently show up at the last possible minute before we were to begin playing. Jack warned me many times, but he had finally had enough. He took me aside one day and told me he had to let me go. He said he had genuine affection for me and that I was very talented, but he had a weak heart and he feared for his health. Still, they weren't about to let a good young musician get away in those days. Jack arranged for my agent to switch me to another hotel that featured a younger bandleader with good blood work.

My memories of the Catskills are very precious to me, and although I performed in the area significantly after its heyday of the 1950s and '60s, I was still in time to witness the last of the glory days, to work with some truly great acts and musicians, and to experience that excitement. It was simply a dream come true in every way imaginable, and I had the time of my life.

Toward the end of my stay, the decline of the area picked up pace. I was moving on to greener pastures for my own reasons, but there was no denying what was happening to my beloved Catskills. For years, there had been talk of gambling coming to rescue the area and its hotels. At each turn, the dream faded. Cheap airline travel to exotic places, Atlantic City, and the breakdown of the nuclear family all contributed to the demise of the Catskills.

Not long ago, I again returned to my old haunts in the Catskills for a documentary that is being filmed about my show. Almost all of the big hotels have been torn down. Others are boarded up. I stood on the stage of the nightclub at Kutshers where I had performed many years earlier as a young drummer in the show band (Kutshers Country Club is still alive and looking grand, albeit only seasonally). It was pretty eerie. Even though I'd been in this room on an empty afternoon getting ready for rehearsals many times in the past, there had always been an expectation in the air . . . a feeling that something exciting was about to happen. Now the room felt used up—as if the spirit was willing, but the body couldn't give anymore. This room, which had seen so many exciting nights, heard so many songs, and been part of so much laughter, was like a grand old southern matron who had lost her wealth, but still held on to her dignity.

After we left, I drove by the Concord and the Laurels. Gone. I stopped by the Pines Hotel in South Fallsburg where Speedy Garfin held sway in the lounge. The heavy steel chain across the front entrance couldn't block out the broken windows and overgrown grounds. The sign still sported the words GATEWAY TO YOUR FABULOUS VACATION. On my journey home, I passed by the decaying and now condemned Red Apple Rest, the place which for decades told generations of vacationers they were indeed halfway to paradise.

I can't help feeling nostalgic and sad for those places and those days, but I know all things pass. People, places, things . . . they all have their time and then make way for the new. It is a bittersweet reality that none of us would change, even if given the choice. *Vos geven iz geven un nito* (What was, was—and is no more). This is the apt title of a famous Yiddish song.

What I can't totally comprehend is what happens to the love, the joy, the laughter, and the other emotions that happened in these places. Where do they go? Are they in the walls or in the air where the buildings stood? Are they still occurring in some alternate universe right next to where I'm standing? I know that the emotions and memories still live inside those of us who experienced them—but is that all? Can walls talk? I thought I could hear them when I stood on stage in the empty nightclub at Kutshers.

Several times in the last few years, when on the site of one of these ruined old hotels or bungalow colonies, I've experienced a strange feeling. As I watch the wind blow across the overgrown fields and ruffle the torn curtains through the broken windows, I imagine I can almost hear the faint sounds of music and laughter.

UNCONTROLLABLE LAUGHTER

(or Laughing at the Worst Possible Times)

*"Laughter can be more satisfying than honor,
more precious than money, more
heart cleansing than prayer."*

—Harriet Rochlin

LAUGHTER IS EXTREMELY IMPORTANT. It releases stress, and it balances our being. It even releases beneficial chemicals into our system from the veritable pharmacy that exists within our bodies. Our state of mind influences our well-being, and laughter is one of the greatest healers. Yet there is a certain type of laughter that is different from the rest. It brings the same benefits, but, because of its intense power, also inherent risks. When it occurs, it is like a simmering volcano that must erupt—and *nothing* can stop it. It is that uncontrollable laughter that hits so infrequently we can recall and treasure the few times we've experienced it. For me, this welcome, but potentially embarrassing, phenomenon has struck about a half dozen times.

I was about four years old the first time. We were still living in the "old neighborhood," and Joanie and I were jumping on one of the beds. We tumbled off the bed together and fell into the large cardboard box that we kept underneath to store shoes. Joanie and I laughed

79

so hard and for so long, that now, almost fifty years later, the memory is still fresh and strong in my mind. Recalling memories from that young an age is usually difficult, but I remember this occasion as though it were yesterday. I remember it somewhere deep in my being, not just intellectually—I can still *feel* it. That is the power and beauty of intense, uncontrollable laughter.

Unfortunately, these eruptions of hilarity can often come at the most inappropriate times and for the most inappropriate reasons. While I'm sure some of you can recall wanting to laugh at the worst possible time, I'm guessing you were able to control it for the most part—or maybe not. I confess to a few occasions when uncontrollable laughter has totally and completely overtaken me.

Rosh Hashanah Services: My dad, my sisters Wanda and Joanie (both relatively functional at the time), Lisa, and my dad's wife Ruth were attending Rosh Hashanah service at our temple. There are many traditions I like about the Jewish faith, but Rosh Hashanah and Yom Kippur are my favorites. Rosh Hashanah literally means "head of the year" and is considered the Jewish New Year. It begins an annual ten-day self-examination and introspection period—the Days of Awe—that culminates in Yom Kippur, a day considered so holy that Jews traditionally fast for atonement. I look inward and self-evaluate all year long, but I truly love this yearly "take stock of your soul and your life" period built into the tradition. Although I do not observe the letter of every Jewish "law," I do exercise the spirit of the law, and I love the spirit of this "law" most of all.

As one might expect, Rosh Hashanah is a pretty serious time—a High Holy Day, in fact—although not quite as serious and somber as Yom Kippur. We were seated near the front of the sanctuary, in about the fourth row. Sitting up front was already a problem for me. In fact, I had always wondered, *What kind of schmuck sits up in the front?* Now I knew: a schmuck whose father is hard of hearing, that's who. And never mind that—to get a seat in the front, you have to arrive like six months before the service begins—to *hold seats* for your family. This is another dicey adventure of spreading out every possible piece of garment that can be used to cover a space in the row.

All seemed to be going pretty well, which was already a blessing considering my sisters were there. Then a young boy—perhaps bar-mitzvah age (thirteen)—began reading from the Torah. It hit me slowly at first. I couldn't help but notice that he had an extremely unusual quality to his voice, sort of like Woody Woodpecker on speed, only funnier. Under normal circumstances, I would perhaps make a mental note and think nothing more of it. You certainly wouldn't call any attention to it. But then, slowly, I began to feel that awful, terrifying feeling that I would start laughing and would be absolutely unable to control it. Fear coursed through my body, and my mind was awhirl. This was definitely not the time or place. But the more I tried to fight it, the funnier it seemed. Aside from the boy's chant, the synagogue was stone silent. *Why did we have to sit so close to the front?!*

Sure enough, it began. I squeezed my finger . . . hard. Then I bit my cheek. Then I bit my tongue. But all this was to no avail. My body started to shake, and various noises began to emanate from my body. Of course my sister Wanda, ever vigilant for anything that might go awry at any time or place, took notice. I saw laughter begin to bubble up inside her as well, and I shot her a stern but pleading look. *Do NOT laugh out loud. Do not even acknowledge me. Look away!* Of course, that only made matters worse. To my horror, she elbowed Joanie and nodded toward me. Joanie, God bless her, never needed much prodding to go off into a good laugh. Now, the three of us were feeding off each other, and our stifled laughter began to emit strange noises eerily reminiscent of the alien language in a Teletubbies TV episode.

I did the only thing I could think of. I covered my head with my tallis—the traditional Jewish prayer shawl worn by men. It is not uncommon, when one is deep in prayer, to pull the tallis over one's head to close out the world for personal meditation. I'm sure that at best I looked like some sort of apoplectic ghost, or at worst, simply what I was—an incredibly immature jerk who was trying to hide his unbelievably inappropriate laughter under his tallis. Of course, by this time, my father had taken notice of what was going on. He whispered his old standby, "What are you, a baby? It's time to grow up!"

As much as I didn't want to embarrass my dad, and as bad as I was feeling about the whole episode, this fit of laughter was really beyond my control, and his admonition to stop only made it worse. My sisters were no help. I finally gathered my courage and did the only honorable thing I could. I got up and left. Right in the middle of the reading. Now, *everyone* saw me leave, and I don't think my attempt at the "I've got to go the men's room immediately" walk fooled anyone, especially since I still had my head covered with a wildly shaking tallis. My sisters stayed, and I later learned that they'd somehow composed themselves. (It's never quite as bad for those who get a contact high as it is for the original host.)

Somehow, out in the lobby, I slowly regained my composure as well. However, I knew any attempt to reenter the sanctuary while this kid was still chanting was out of the question. It can take quite a while to fully recover after one of these episodes, and there is a distinct danger of relapse at any moment. It's similar to a seizure of sorts—it's best to keep the patient calm.

By the time I returned, the young man had thankfully stopped reading. He was, however, still seated up on the bimah—the honored platform where the Torahs are kept—but this I could bear. He didn't *look* funny, he just *sounded* funny.

When the service moved on, the boy left the bimah and headed for his seat. God must have been having some fun with me that day, because the boy and his entire family were sitting directly in the row behind us! There is simply no way the family had not noticed the ruckus taking place right in front of them. I felt terrible! I never intended to make anybody feel bad—I wasn't even really laughing at him (although his voice *was* really funny). It was just one of those stupid inexplicable things—like maybe I ate some bad gefilte fish the night before or something. The kid's chanting was simply the catalyst—he was just the innocent bystander in a "drive-by" laughing.

After service, when we arrived at my dad's house for lunch, I was flooded with a litany of his greatest hits: *Are you a child? What is the matter with you? You're wild!* And a reprise of the ever popular, *It's time to grow up!* Of course, my dad was right. I'd behaved awfully. Joanie and Wanda were having a ball watching me "get it"—the "fair-haired wonder boy" was in trouble, and they were beside themselves with merriment. I notice my father didn't say anything to them—*hey, they'd been laughing, too!* It was no use, we all knew I was the culprit. All I could do was apologize profusely. I tried my best to explain that this was some kind of nervous tic or something, and when it hit, I simply couldn't control it, no matter what I did.

Anyhow, this was really bad, and I had to make amends, especially as this was the season of repentance. I called the rabbi, who I was sure must have noticed the entire escapade. We were, after all, in the fourth row! Come to think of it, this whole situation was partly my dad's fault. Had we been seated in back, where normal people sit— this whole thing could have been avoided! After some consideration, I decided not to take the argument in that direction. My gentle rabbi assured me he had no idea what I was talking about, he hadn't noticed any commotion during the service. However, he'd be glad to give me the family's contact info, so that I might call and apologize. Sure.

I waited a few days, then summoned all my courage and called: *"Hi, it's Jake Ehrenreich, Shana Tova."* (Good New Year.)

My family is pretty well known in the community, so I didn't really have to explain who I was.

"Oh . . . hello," was her less than enthusiastic response. My luck, I had to get the mother.

"Well," I continued, *"perhaps you might have noticed some disturbance coming from my area during the Rosh Hashanah service."*

Silence.

"I wanted to explain that I unfortunately have a very rare ailment— really, the doctors don't know what it is—that comes over me periodically. It's some sort of uncontrollable affectation really, a kind of tic—very troublesome and embarrassing for me and my family. I'm so sorry it happened during your son's reading."

Silence.

I continued. *"I just wanted to assure you it had nothing to do with Vinnie's* [not his real name] *beautiful leining* [chanting from the

READER/CUSTOMER CARE SURVEY

We care about your opinions! Please take a moment to fill out our online Reader Survey at **http://survey.hcibooks.com**.
As a **"THANK YOU"** you will receive a **VALUABLE INSTANT COUPON** towards future book purchases
as well as a **SPECIAL GIFT** available only online! Or, you may mail this card back to us.

(PLEASE PRINT IN ALL CAPS)

First Name		MI.	Last Name

Address			City

State	Zip	Email

1. Gender
❏ Female   ❏ Male

2. Age
❏ 8 or younger
❏ 9-12   ❏ 13-16
❏ 17-20   ❏ 21-30
❏ 31+

3. Did you receive this book as a gift?
❏ Yes   ❏ No

4. Annual Household Income
❏ under $25,000
❏ $25,000 - $34,999
❏ $35,000 - $49,999
❏ $50,000 - $74,999
❏ over $75,000

5. What are the ages of the children living in your house?
❏ 0 - 14   ❏ 15+

6. Marital Status
❏ Single
❏ Married
❏ Divorced
❏ Widowed

7. How did you find out about the book?
(please choose one)
❏ Recommendation
❏ Store Display
❏ Online
❏ Catalog/Mailing
❏ Interview/Review

8. Where do you usually buy books?
(please choose one)
❏ Bookstore
❏ Online
❏ Book Club/Mail Order
❏ Price Club (Sam's Club, Costco's, etc.)
❏ Retail Store (Target, Wal-Mart, etc.)

9. What subject do you enjoy reading about the most?
(please choose one)
❏ Parenting/Family
❏ Relationships
❏ Recovery/Addictions
❏ Health/Nutrition
❏ Christianity
❏ Spirituality/Inspiration
❏ Business Self-help
❏ Women's Issues
❏ Sports

10. What attracts you most to a book?
(please choose one)
❏ Title
❏ Cover Design
❏ Author
❏ Content

TAPE IN MIDDLE; DO NOT STAPLE

BUSINESS REPLY MAIL
FIRST-CLASS MAIL   PERMIT NO 45   DEERFIELD BEACH, FL

POSTAGE WILL BE PAID BY ADDRESSEE

Health Communications, Inc.
3201 SW 15th Street
Deerfield Beach FL 33442-9875

FOLD HERE

Comments

torah], *and I wanted to sincerely apologize to you all in case it was at all distracting."*

At this point I should explain that although it seems like I was not telling the truth, I was . . . mostly. While it might have been Germaine's (not his real name) voice that started me laughing, the force of the episode was not his doing—so, technically, I wasn't really laughing at him. Anyway, I always thought that white lies that spare someone's feelings are good things. For instance, let's say you know your wife shopped all week for a dress for the big ball, and she found one at the last minute. She walks into the living room while you're innocently perusing the Arts and Leisure section of the Sunday *New York Times* in your house robe and she says, "Do I look fat in this?" Explain to me how telling a little white lie in that instance is not a mitzvah (good deed). But I digress.

"Uh huh," was the mom's response to my detailed and thoughtful explanation of what had transpired. It didn't seem like she was buying any of it—which is actually quite insensitive, now that I think about it. What if I *did* really have a strange medical condition that no one had ever heard of before? I mean, I didn't—but I *could* have.

I sucked it up. *"Well, again, let me wish you and your family a healthy, prosperous and happy year for you all."*

I hung up. It didn't go so well, but I made a reasonable effort. I thought that was a pretty good story. She could have at least acknowledged *that*. At the very least, I was able to quell the urge to say, *"Hey, I'm really sorry folks, but face it, your son seems like a nice kid, but his voice is ridiculously hysterical. Tell me the truth, you didn't want to laugh? Come on, you should have read some sort of disclaimer or something before he started. . . . "*

I learned a valuable lesson that day. If I'm ever in temple, and I see that kid headed for the bimah, I'm headed for the door. I know I may not sound appropriately contrite, but at least the kid himself didn't hear us laughing, it was only his family—and they didn't even care about my rare illness! In the scheme of things, I still think I'm one of the good guys, so I cut myself some slack.

The Bar Mitzvah Celebration: From the time I was about fifteen years old, I played in bands for private events like weddings and bar mitzvah celebrations—and I continued that for many years when I was not working elsewhere. At one bar mitzvah party I played (I must have been in my late twenties), the boy becoming a bar mitzvah was a clarinet player. The plan was that sometime during the afternoon celebration, he would play some selections on his clarinet, accompanied by our keyboard player.

This was a kind, gentle family, and they were hosting a tasteful celebration. They even gave the band their own table near the front of the room, which was very thoughtful. At the appropriate time, Vito (not his real name) was announced onto the stage to play. I took my seat at the band table to eat my fruit cup . . . right beside the bandstand.

It started off innocently enough. Tony (not his real name) began to play and was actually a fairly accomplished musician for his age. The family and guests were *kvelling* (showing great pride). Then, the trouble began: "SQUEAK!"

If you've never heard a clarinet squeak, trust me when I say it happens to be one of the world's funniest, quirkiest sounds. It's not even so much the sound itself, it's just that it comes from absolutely nowhere. You'll be listening to the nice music . . . la dee dah . . . then, without any warning, SQUEAK! It's so abrupt . . . it's like sitting on a whoopee cushion. It just makes you jump out of your seat. But then it happens over and over with no warning in between. No matter— any *normal* adult would just take these squeaks in stride as a young musician's learning process and enjoy the performance. Unless, of course, it was one of those rare times when that usually mature, upstanding, *normal* adult felt that pent-up volcano of laughter bubbling to the surface, just ready to explode, with no power on earth strong enough to stop it . . . in that case, each "SQUEAK" becomes a death knell.

Of course, the worst part about the squeaking was that I never knew when it was about to happen. I was already so on edge that each time a squeak sounded, I felt the unbearable rush of lava-laughter bubble up inside me. I panicked. I realized I would soon erupt like Mount Etna. Fortunately, it wasn't as quiet as a synagogue, but my immaturity would soon be on display for all to see, as the laughter ultimately "possessed" me. Wait! That's it! . . . It was a *possession*! If only this were a communion instead of a bar mitzvah, I might have stood a fair chance of a quick back-room exorcism. No luck here— I looked around in desperation, but to my disappointment, everyone's collars faced the right direction. Leaving the room didn't seem to be an option, so I chose the only other available course of action: I slowly slid down my chair and disappeared under the table.

Musicians are always looking for a practical joke, and they never let you get away with anything. I tried my best to pretend I wasn't there, but they would have none of it.

"Hey, man, what are you doing under the table? Are you . . . cracking up? Come up here . . . come on, man!"

I simply couldn't control my laughter. I spent the rest of the performance under the table, praying for the kid to get his chops together.

Later on, I apologetically told Christopher's (not his real name) parents that a severe stomachache had overcome me during the performance, and not knowing what else to do, I simply had gone under the table to wait it out. Thankfully, they didn't even know what I was talking about—and I believed them.

Mercifully I personally haven't had an attack or "possession" like this in some time (but I may be due soon!), but I enjoyed being the catalyst for one not long ago. I was speaking as a presenter at a weekend symposium of worldwide journalists, gathered in upstate New York for a serious discussion of art and media and their role in the new world of emerging technologies. As usual, I tossed a few jokes into my presentation. Later, one of the attendees—a serious Washington D.C.–investigative journalist—told me that she and a colleague had laughed so hard at one of the jokes that they just couldn't stop laughing—long after it was still appropriate. As they laughed through serious parts of my presentation, they felt like the bad kids in school as they avoided the angry stares from those around them (which only made them laugh more!). I got great satisfaction out of this; something I did or said had triggered a glorious and rare laugh-your-head-off moment for them, and I knew I would always be associated with that fond memory.

I know how strong a memory like that can be. Regardless of their odd circumstances, all of these memories cause me to smile. But the strongest by far is the memory of that long ago moment with Joanie—now gone and buried—and the joyous uncontrollable laughter we shared. That laughter touched a place deep inside of me and left an indelible mark on my soul. I can feel it as I write this. *Nothing* can ever take that memory from me, and I will cherish it always.

JOANIE

(or A Celebration of Innocence and Love)

"Be a life long or short, its completeness
depends on what it was lived for."

—David Starr Jordan

DEATH IS A DESTINATION we all share, and as much as we avoid thinking about it, it is always there to remind us of what life is about. When a person's life ends—especially a loved one—we, the living, are forced to examine what ultimately remains from that life. Sometimes, it is hard to do in the fog of grief—and in the case of an untimely passing, even more difficult. Yet, perhaps there really are no untimely passings. We are each given our own unique journey to travel and our own time to say what we're here to say.

I was in the midst of composing my sister Joanie's eulogy when I began to shift my view of what I thought her life had been about. Attempting to sum up someone's life in a few pages forces you to focus on only the essential, transcendent elements. In a way, writing about Joanie was simple, because she was simple—uncomplicated in her view of the world. I easily referred to Joanie as an angel on Earth, because of the angelic traits she exhibited in life. In the deepest sense, Joanie was without guile. I slowly began to realize that what I thought was a sad, lonely, wasted life was actually a journey that spread joy and celebrated innocence and love.

Joanie—named Yochewet Liba—was the middle kid, and she had all the stereotypical personality traits. She was insecure and was never quite sure that she was loved as much as the eldest and the youngest. She felt this most acutely with my dad, since he was the main disciplinarian, and she never got hit as a kid. She interpreted this to mean that he didn't care about her as much as he cared for Wanda and me. Of course, it wasn't that my dad didn't love her—it was simply that she had the "misfortune" of being a good kid. (Had I known this was going on, I'd have done something bad and blamed it on her.)

Joanie was born in a displaced persons camp in Germany just after the war. She was only six months old when she arrived in the United States with my parents and Wanda. My family came by plane because Joanie was too young to make the usual ocean voyage (which would have taken them through Ellis Island). When they arrived, they were housed in a homeless shelter in Manhattan for survivors of the Nazi Holocaust in Europe.

Joanie was blonde and fair like my mom, in stark contrast to my sister Wanda and me, who were dark like my dad. My mom used to say that Joanie was like her and that Wanda and I were like my dad. Joanie didn't like that comparison too much, because my father was the powerhouse intellectual, and we all knew my mom had some issues.

Because Joanie was closer in age to me than Wanda (only seven years as opposed to twelve), she and I had a much closer relationship during our early years. Joanie had an even temperament, and I looked up to her, and we were often allies in our feuds against Wanda. She was the kind who would get you four different Hallmark cards for your birthday, and her room was filled with plaques featuring sappy expressions of love. I always thought it was cool that she seemed so into love. Although we loved each other in my family, we didn't say it much. I guess Joanie needed it more than Wanda and myself . . . more like my mom. Ironically, the translation of Joanie's middle name is "love."

Joanie was a bright, happy kid. Then she had a very unfortunate experience sometime during her early years in grade school. I was pretty young at the time, and it was mostly hidden from me (as many things were in those days), so I don't know exactly what happened, but I know the outcome and the ramifications of this event on Joanie's life. Joanie had had some sort of "episode"—that's what they called it, but I never really understood exactly what it was. She didn't have a seizure or a blackout—just an "episode." I guess it must have taken place at school. I believe the doctors did some tests and promptly pronounced that she had epilepsy. They prescribed Dilantin and Phenobarbitol— powerful drugs for a young kid—supposedly to control her seizures. However, she had not had any seizures, nor did she have any later in life. Believing they were doing what was necessary for their child, my parents followed the doctor's orders. Joanie stayed on these drugs for two decades before being told by another doctor that she did not have epilepsy. If you're wondering, Dilantin accumulates in the brain causing atrophy of the cerebellum. Phenobarbital is a barbiturate (depressant or downer) with sedative and hypnotic properties, which causes depression of the central nervous system. I wonder what my parents would have thought had they known that Phenobarbital was the drug used by Nazi doctors to "remove" children with disease and deformities from the population. I believe that two decades of these drugs, smack in the middle of Joanie's developmental years, played a significant role in destroying her chance for a normal life.

Perhaps Joanie's experience in the medical system influences my attitude toward doctors' pronouncements today. I'm respectful, aware, and skeptical—especially when it comes to giving anyone in our family drugs, and we always ask many questions and seek out any natural alternatives for all our health-care decisions. Surprisingly, Joanie landed on the other end of the spectrum. Any suggestion that a doctor of hers might be capable of a mistake or in any way be less than 100-percent perfect and infallible drew a sharp rebuke. She once confided in me that she *needed* to believe they were right. When I asked why, I received a stonewall answer: "I just *need* to, that's all." I think that acknowledging that the sedation of her entire youth was due to a mistake would have been too much for Joanie's fragile constitution to handle. So, she protected herself with her belief. Even when she was later told by other doctors that her diagnosis had indeed been in error, and even when those doctors who finally removed her from her medications did so cold turkey, and she had to be sent to the emergency room in withdrawal—even then, she still never acknowledged the possibility of a doctor's fallibility.

While I know doctors do their best, I'm still angry over my sister's treatment in the medical system. But Joanie wasn't. Because that's who Joanie was. She wouldn't allow herself to bear a grudge or harbor ill will. Somehow, miraculously, through all of her difficulties, and even through two decades of sedation, Joanie's bubbling and loving personality always came through.

Joanie was deeply loved by the patients in the dental office where she worked as a hygienist. Many of them were very upset when Joanie got ill, and I continued to receive phone calls from them to see how she was doing for many years. Joanie had been a dental hygienist in a Brooklyn practice that featured an almost exclusively African-American clientele. Her genuine purity and goodness and innocence created a beautiful "color blind" love between her and her patients even during a very difficult period of racial strife in our country.

I can only imagine how Joanie might have turned out, and what her life may have been, if given a fair chance. During a recent performance run of my show, I was contacted by an old friend of Joanie's. She had seen an article in the newspaper that featured a family photo and recognized Joanie. She left a phone message to tell me she would be attending the show and to check if there were any performances when Joanie might be there as well. When I finally got the courage to call her back, she went on and on about how much she loved Joanie, and how loving and genuine she was, and how helpful and selfless my sister had been to her in a difficult time of her life. She was so excited at the prospect of seeing her again. It was all I could do to tell her that Joanie had passed away. We cried together, and I told her how grateful I was to hear what she said about Joanie. I had spoken similarly at her funeral.

Joanie was diagnosed with early-onset Alzheimer's disease sometime in her midforties, even younger than my mother before her and my sister Wanda after. As always, we tried alternative methods of treatment as well as standard methods. Watching her decline in the prime of life was unbelievably sad and frustrating. Yet Joanie kept a bright spirit alive even during the most trying times. She was always ready with a smile or a laugh—and she never minded being on the receiving end of a joke. In later years, there were some sweet comical moments that I still cherish.

For instance, at a Passover dinner a number of years back, my father was retelling the story of the exodus from Egypt and the overall Passover story, as is the custom on that holiday. At one point, he looked directly at Joanie during the reading. Thinking he was directing his gaze to her purposely because she might not understand, she responded, "I know Dad, I saw the movie!" (The movie *The Ten Commandments* for which Charlton Heston is famous for playing Moses is the story of the exodus from Egypt.)

We ended up placing Joanie in an adult home near the area where my dad and I live. Unfortunately, within a year or so, she had to be moved to the nursing facility on the same grounds. I'd sing to her during our visits, just as I had to my mom, although Joanie loved the Beatles, so the repertoire was different. (But once in a while I'd stick in a Yiddish song from our childhood, just for kicks.) When the weather was nice out, we would walk around the grounds holding hands; sometimes, I wheeled her in her chair. As with Wanda later, people thought Joanie was my mother although she was barely fifty years old. As time progressed, Joanie had to have restraints put on her chair, so as not to slide off and injure herself. I was desperate not to lose her. We tried all sorts of treatments and medications, and when all seemed lost, we even tried electroshock therapy to try to "reboot" her brain. Notwithstanding our efforts, in the end, Joanie was simply curled up in a fetal position—just like mom—when I would visit.

As you might imagine, seeing my beautiful sister Joanie in this situation was very difficult emotionally, and I deeply sympathize with all those who are faced with similar situations. There's an intense feeling of hopelessness and sadness that accompanies the mental unraveling of a loved one that is hard to convey to someone who hasn't experienced it. It almost seems as if the person you knew is gone, although they're right in front of you. You can sometimes see the inner turmoil and confusion in their years, as if a veil of darkness they can't pierce had descended over them.

Just before visits, I would try to enter an emotional place that allowed me to exude an attitude of joy and warmth. I didn't want to show up bringing the energy of pity and sadness. But after the visit, I'd feel emotionally depleted, and I would often have to sit in the car for a while before driving away, just to compose myself. I worked hard on finding ways and techniques to stay in the joy of life and to strike a balance by staying focused on the things for which I'm grateful. But, sometimes, I'd simply skip visits for periods of time because I just couldn't get myself to go.

I had thought for a long time that Joanie's life was failed and wasted. She never married, had few adult relationships—male or female—and ultimately ended up living with my sister Wanda, watching TV, and smoking cigarettes in her last years before having to move to the home. But Joanie always kept a smile on her face as long as she could. I see in my mind's eye my wonderful and loving sister, and I recall the vibrant young girl with so much promise, and it still makes me very sad—partly because of the mistakes that were made, but mostly because she's not here to share my life. Not here to be a sister or a loving aunt for my son. They would have liked each other.

When reviewing Joanie's life for her eulogy, and in speaking about

her during the week of mourning, I realized that if we measured her life not in terms of its accomplishments or duration, but in terms of its beauty and its capacity for love and honesty, then Joanie's life was a huge success. We always search to say something kind about people when they die. In Joanie's case, the thoughts came easily to my mind and the words passed effortlessly from my lips.

My sister Joanie was fifty-five years old when she died. I know she always wanted to do good, so I asked to have her organs donated for someone else to use. I thought this would be a fitting last act for Joanie. Because of her Alzheimer's disease, her organs were refused for donation. Her body would go back to its maker whole, but maybe that was fitting after all. For me, it was just a final heartbreaking moment in my beautiful sister's life.

SEX
(or It's My Thousandth Time, Too)

"I chased a girl for two years only to discover
that her tastes were exactly like mine:
We were both crazy about girls."

—Groucho Marx

WHEN **I** WAS A KID, TWO MAJOR things shouted "American" to me: sports and music. Because I excelled at both, this led to social popularity. Although I loved sports and had even dreamed of someday making a career out of it, I realized pretty early on that being a musician was powerfully alluring to the opposite sex. And being popular with "chicks" was the ultimate validation of my Americanism, or so I thought. This would prove to be an important part of my wayward journey of self-discovery, which continued throughout my twenties. Because I was "gigging" as a musician at a very early age, "opportunities"—which I wouldn't have had otherwise—presented themselves to me rather frequently.

Virtually everyone remembers their first time, but I also vividly recall my "almost" first time. I was doing a gig in the Catskill Mountains at the Ridge Mountain Hotel in Parksville, New York. (That was the summer I also attended sleepaway camp. That's how young I was.) A guest, who was at least eighteen, invited me up to her room. Like everyone else, she assumed I was much older than I was. When I got to her room, she made every attempt to seduce me, but being as nervous as I was, I pretended to read the newspaper. She even went as far as caressing my "boyhood" through my pants, and I was *terrified*. I had no idea what to do, so I just continued to pretend to read. The words on the page were a blur. She finally got so fed up with me that she angrily proclaimed I was probably a virgin anyway and kicked me out. Of course she was right.

I ran to the phone booth and called my best friend, Andy, back in Brooklyn to tell him about the girl who wanted to have sex with me. Freaking out on the other end, he asked what happened. "Well, I called to tell you about it," I explained. That's when it hit me what a putz I was.

Success followed a year or so later when I was working at another Catskills hotel called the Melbourne in Ellenville. (Since I was fifteen, I had to lie about my age to get the gig.) The band was sitting around the lobby after the show, and it was pretty late. One of the female guests had started hanging around with us; perhaps you could call her our groupie. We got on the topic of sex, as usual, and this quite attractive young woman admitted to being a virgin. The bandleader, Doug, who was twenty, told her that nineteen is too old to still be a virgin and tried to convince her she should rectify that . . . with him. The desk clerk, another lowlife, totally agreed that her predicament was unacceptable and offered up an empty guest room in support. It was like a telethon. The guys made it seem like a charity fund-raiser for a worthy cause. Doug was making the logical case that as an older and wiser person, he would be willing to show her the ropes so she'd have a good sexual foundation for the rest of her life—or some such ridiculousness. (I really think horny guys will say just about anything that comes to their minds and see where it leads them.) In this novel gambit, he was casting himself as some sort of philanthropist who was willing do her a favor. If nothing else, it was certainly creative.

She was resistant at first, then suddenly seemed to have an epiphany. "Okay!" she said. "I'll do it, but I'll only go with him." She pointed right at me.

My eyes widened and my heart skipped a beat. Hey, I'd just been sitting there minding my own business! I felt flattered and kind of special, but it definitely took me by surprise. *Who, me?* I hemmed and hawed a bit, but there was no getting out of this with my manhood in tact if I refused. I didn't want the guys to know I was a virgin.

Good to his word, the clerk offered up the keys to the honeymoon suite. I was nervous, but also really excited . . . this was it! I was trying my best to stay cool and keep up a calm exterior. We went up to the room, and we somehow figured out how to do it. Neither one of us had a clue, but I pretended like I'd done it a million times before. It was sweet.

When it was over, it felt so special and homey that I decided she deserved to know the truth. As we lay there in the afterglow, I whispered in her ear, "It's my first time, too."

She shot straight up in bed and promptly proceeded to freak out. "What?!" she yelled. "What do you mean, your first time?!"

The anger on her face shouted even louder than her words, and I knew I had made a huge mistake. She couldn't bear the thought that her first time wasn't with an experienced man.

In one of *the* greatest saves of all time, I thought quickly and said,

"My first time with a virgin, I mean."

"Oh! Your first time with a virg—I understand." She let out a huge sigh of relief, settled down, and was quite content once again.

The genie was out of the bottle. She came back to my room the next morning, then later in the afternoon, then again after dinner, and then after the show, too. It must have been my vast sexual prowess, technique, and experience—yeah, or maybe not. After that week, we lost track of each other, although I once thought I saw her working in an optical store in Kings Plaza in Brooklyn. She never did end up learning the truth about my virginity, and I still regret we couldn't share that "first-time" bond together.

Being a musician laid the foundation for all of my sexual escapades, and I took total advantage of it. As it turned out, the genie was out of the bottle for me, too.

My next "opportunity" soon arrived. My friend Jack and I were doing a keyboard and drums gig at a singles dance at a fancy hotel in Manhattan (we should have called our group "A Pair of Jacks"). We were still too young to drive, so we took a car service to the gig from Brooklyn. At the end of the night, we were waiting in the coffee shop of the hotel for the car to come, when three pretty young blondes at the other table said, "Sorry you boys have to leave."

That got my attention quick. I was young—not stupid.

They were tourists on their last night and were looking for some "fun." I took down their room number and told them we had to drop our instruments back at our place, but we'd be back and they should wait.

In the car on the way back to Brooklyn, I begged Jack to come back to Manhattan with me.

"My parents would kill me," he whined.

"This is the opportunity of a lifetime," I tried to convince him. "These things don't happen every day! It's like getting Mickey Mantle's autograph!"

There was no budging him. I, on the other hand, saw this as an amazing opportunity and wouldn't allow it to pass me by. I was not about to repeat the whole newspaper-reading fiasco, but I was very conflicted—would I really do this alone? Looking back, I must have had pretty big cojones. I was a little *pisher*, and these were three somewhat older (maybe twenty?) aggressive chicks. They might have been hookers (or guys) for all I knew back then, but it didn't even cross my mind. All I knew was, I could go for it, or I could wimp out and just tell a good story of what might have been. Ultimately, I was just too dumb to know what I shouldn't do. I took the subway back to Manhattan from Brooklyn at 2:00 AM by myself to meet these chicks. I must have been out of my mind. I never even took the subway into Manhattan during the day! How did I know they would still be waiting for me at the hotel? How did I know I wouldn't get lost—or mugged—or killed! As I always say, motivation is everything.

I told my parents I was sleeping at Jack's house and prayed they wouldn't call. I had that feeling of power you get when you commit to something big. I was going for it, and if I got caught, I got caught. I felt very grown-up, and I was not going to let a little thing like my parents stand in the way of my decision.

When I got to the girls' hotel room, they were pretty hammered. Before I knew it, the three of them were all over me, pulling at my clothes, caressing me, and kissing my neck. Having the three of them all over me was a dream come true, but I was completely overwhelmed and suggested one at a time would be better. *Putz!*

I spent a crazy night with them, and then became their tourist play-thing for the next day. Much of the day's details are lost to antiquity, but the girls were pretty wild, and the one thing that stands out in my mind was getting felt up in the pews of Saint Patrick's Cathedral. I'm sure that can't be right. Now I know what "Catholic guilt" feels like.

My first "long-term" relationship came along a few years later, when I was nineteen. I was renting a bungalow in a colony owned by a jazz musician, and all the renters were single male musicians working at the local hotels. One afternoon, a beautiful blonde showed up in a low-cut blouse and short cut-off jeans. You might ask, "Did this attract the attention of the residents?" To which I would retort, *"Is a snake's ass close to the ground?"* The guys were like a pack of hyenas fighting over a single morsel of food. But when the water cleared, I somehow wound up on top (pun intended), and the blonde just stayed.

As I left for my gig that night, I asked, "Will you be here when I get back?"

She replied, "Do you want me to?"

And I said, "Yeah."

This went on for a year and a half.

She was thirty, and having a hot older woman hot for me was the ultimate fulfillment of a wild fantasy, and it opened up a whole new world for me. She taught me to be more attentive to a woman's needs as well as many other things.

One evening, as I was getting amorous with her, she whispered, "No, stop."

So I stopped, and she looked puzzled.

"What are you doing?" she asked.

"You said stop," I replied.

"Don't be an idiot," she said.

It seemed there was *a lot* to learn.*

I had told her I was twenty-seven, and she was even a bit upset about being *three* years older than me. When she finally took a good look at my driver's license, her head spun around *Exorcist*-style. We ended up staying together for a while longer, and then finally had a mutual breakup—although we stayed friends for many years.

Anyhow, after that relationship, I went back on the prowl, and upon seeing a pretty woman, any pretty woman, I put my charm to work. Sometimes I struck out, but most times I didn't, and overall, I became a pretty successful womanizer who was always on the lookout for some action. Between "conquests," I'd briefly wonder where this path would lead me, but, honestly, I was having too much fun to worry about it. Even my family knew I was successful with women, and it was a point of pride with me. It seemed cool, like the old movies—I felt like I fit in.

Once, I was staying at a small hotel in France for a few weeks. I was intrigued by the truly adorable desk clerk. When she was on duty, I'd flirt with her. But because I didn't speak French and she didn't speak much English, it was difficult for us to communicate. One evening, I came in fairly late to find her on the night shift. I turned on my charm and began my usual carousing. This time she got very serious, looked at me intensely, and said in broken English, "What you want from me?"

In no way is this meant to imply that men should ignore women when they say no to their advances. Sex between two consulting adults in a relationship is a different matter and game-playing roles is not the same as not respecting one's wishes.

This caught me a little off guard; she usually just laughed and smiled a lot. I stammered a little and said I wanted her to join me for lunch or something. I'm quite certain she understood "lunch," but then she repeated her question and said some other stuff. I said I didn't understand. Becoming clearly frustrated by my apparent stupidity, she whirled around the desk, took my hand, yanked me into the back office, and shut the door. She slowly and seductively pulled off her sweater revealing an ample young figure and planted her lips on mine for a passionate kiss. She pulled away for a moment, looked me directly in the eye, and said, "Now you understand?"

It's amazing how every time I thought I finally knew the score, some woman would come along and convince me I was still a putz. (If you're wondering, my wife, Lisa, has succeeded in totally convincing me.)

Ah . . . youth. I've chosen to tell some fairly early and sweet formative stories from my life of amorous adventures. The details of my later single life are not really important (and the movie based on that book would have to be rated differently). Suffice it to say, I identified with the pick-up artist I'd become and took pride in my accomplishments. I was great at picking up women on the street, and I'd even go as far as hitting on them in restaurants if their dates got up to go to the bathroom.

Quite honestly, I truly felt like an all-American boy who was single and available with motive and opportunity. I never became addicted to sex, as some people are—for me, it was the chase and the game and the conquest. This behavior was still about fitting in, acting cool, and being accepted. I was on my journey of self-discovery, and I was simply happy to be away from my family, who were off in another world—or I was. The time I spent pursuing women was a way to distract myself from the personal work I needed to do to develop myself further as a human being. Many of us resist that—some people become obsessed with cleaning, some watch television all day, some abuse drugs or alcohol. Me? I mostly picked up chicks.

I ultimately came to see that there were no real answers there for me, but this was part of a search for myself that continued through my twenties and early thirties. As I matured, I started to spend more time finding out who I was internally. But to be totally fair, my womanizing led me to some wonderful people and relationships over the years. I'm grateful for my early and varied opportunities—they taught me a lot. And in many ways, my experiences were very valuable when I finally decided to settle down. I never felt like I missed out on anything, and I learned for sure that my self-worth cannot be found in the thrill of a new conquest.

My friend Dave really put it best: "Wouldn't it be great," he said, "to meet some hot chick in a hotel bar, really hit it off, have some great flirty and suggestive conversation, progress to a few stolen kisses, finally make your way up to her room, slip the key into the door—and as soon as you open it, shake hands and say, *Wow, that was great!* Because, it's all downhill from there anyway."

Ah, the old days . . . funny, but if I followed his advice, I wouldn't be so happily married today. Nonetheless, for many years, my search for answers continued.

I started early!

WANDA
(or Being Responsible for Who We Are)

"We don't see things as they are,
we see things as we are."

—Anais Nin

WHILE **I** HAVE ALWAYS LOVED HER, "angry" and "volatile" are two words I would use to describe my sister Wanda. She was also negative and overbearing. (She probably just needed more love.) We all know how difficult it is to be around people like that. They drain us of our energy and can be vexations to the soul. I sometimes wonder if people are born that way or if circumstances conspire to push them there. Probably either or both can be true, but in the final analysis, I believe we are all ultimately responsible for our own experience—for our outlook and for what we make of our lives—despite our challenges.

Wanda didn't have an easy start. She was born in a Siberian work camp during World War II with mastoiditis (an infection of the mastoid bone of the skull) and underwent a brain operation at six days old . . . with no anesthetic. No wonder she was angry! She was six years old when my family arrived in the United States (six years before I was born). Being the first child of an immigrant family in a new land,

107

my sister had it tough. My parents didn't yet know the culture, so she did all the heavy lifting that paved the way for Joanie and me.

Wanda never really fit in and didn't do well in school. She spoke only Yiddish when she first arrived, so that must have added to her challenge. She eventually fell in with a pretty rough crowd—the "greasers" or "hitters" as they were called. She always liked to tell the story of when she took me to a schoolyard rumble in my baby carriage and some of the boys hid me down a cellar during the fight. That always reminded me of *West Side Story*. In a way, Wanda seemed proud of it, but I always wondered what the heck I was doing there! Where was my mother? Wanda said my mom left me in her care quite often. Who knows, Wanda probably resented having to drag her baby brother around at all. I can't say I blame her.

By the time high school rolled around, Wanda was cutting class all the time. My mom was afraid to tell my dad, so she called our "Aunt Anna" for advice. Aunt Anna had helped sponsor my family to come to this country, for which we will always be grateful. She was native born in the United States, and we all looked up to her and loved her as the ultimate expert in all things American. She said it would be best not to tell my father that Wanda had been cutting classes; he had enough to worry about. I'm sure she meant well, but this came back to haunt our family for years to come. By the time my father found out what was going on, Wanda had dropped out of high school. My father deeply valued education, and I don't think he ever forgave my mother, Aunt Anna, or Wanda for this, and it was the source of intense arguments for many years to come.

Having two older sisters was cool, and I discovered early on that I loved the heart-pounding thrills I got from teasing them, sometimes relentlessly. For instance, one of my favorite pastimes was running into their bedroom while they were watching TV, turning it off, and then dashing away. One of them would have to get up to turn it back on. (At the time, "remote controls" were still a thing of science fiction.) They'd yell all sorts of threats at me and turn the TV back on. Then, I'd wait for them to get comfortable and do it again. This could go on a dozen or more times. (Hey, I had a lot of energy!) It really is a wonder I survived childhood at all, and in fact, the day did come when Wanda decided she'd had enough and tried to do away with me for good.

After a particularly energetic Sunday afternoon of this annoying routine, Wanda threatened that if I did it again, she would kill me . . . seriously. Of course, that didn't stop me. Good to her word, Wanda ran into the kitchen and came out with a huge kitchen knife.

With a racing heart that felt strangely good (like in the Chinese Lots), I ran into the bathroom where I holed up for a while, all the time taunting her, "Nah, nah, you can't get me." She warned that I'd better stay in that bathroom for the rest of my life, because if I came out, my life was over. (Telling the story now, I'm actually on her side.)

As it happened, the one bathroom in our house was directly across from my bedroom. I waited until I was pretty sure the coast was clear, and in a feat of great daring, I shot across the hallway into my bedroom, laughing and taunting all the way, and barricaded myself inside. Wanda was none too happy with this turn of events, and her wrath grew even stronger. I could hear her yelling at Joanie to help her get me.

My next move was the *pièce de résistance*. My room was on the second floor of our house and had a small window overlooking the side alley. Beneath it, an awning covered the door to the downstairs rental apartment. I'd never attempted this before, but I was on a roll. I climbed out of the window, onto the awning, and soon I was safely in the side alley. I ran around to the front of house and up the steps, rang the doorbell, then ran back down the steps and waited. When Wanda answered the door, I gave her my best "Nah, nah, you can't catch me!"

That was the last straw. With kitchen knife in hand, she ran down the steps and into the street in her house robe, screaming, "I'll kill you!" all the way. I took off down the block, with a mixture of fear and exhilaration. Joanie came outside, too, I guess in some sort of support role, but I'm not sure whose side she was on. When it became clear Wanda would never catch me, she turned on Joanie. "It's your fault for not helping me get him!" Now, she started to chase *her* down the block.

Today, we'd all be in juvenile hall.

Although she was wide-eyed and crazy-looking chasing me down that street, Wanda was actually very attractive. She developed early and looked like a cross between Sophia Loren and Audrey Hepburn. Men wanted to date her, but to her, each one was a schmuck. Her self-esteem was so low, I think she reasoned that if a guy wanted her, he'd have to be a loser. Although she enjoyed the companionship of some close girlfriends, she never had good relationships with men. There was one relationship with a guy that got serious, though, but my father didn't approve. He wanted her to get married (and this was a constant cause of fights in our house), just not to him. She ended up breaking it off and wound up being very alone for the rest of her life.

It's likely that some of Wanda's emotional issues came from her relationship with my father. They never got along, and there was always a lot of screaming and yelling in my house. Although she was difficult, she always craved his approval, which she never ended up getting. And Wanda was especially hard on my mom. During fights, she'd curse at her in the worst way and tell her she hoped she'd die. My mother never got over that and even remembered it when she'd forgotten most everything else during her struggle with Alzheimer's disease.

But that was the damaged side of Wanda. Fortunately, she had another side, too. She could be generous, loving, and upbeat.

Once, I brought home a stray dog (the first of many). It was a sweet black dog I named Sunday, because that was the day I found him. I can still see his sweet, trusting face now. My mom wouldn't allow me to keep him, and although I begged and cried, I just couldn't convince her. My sisters tried to help, but my mom simply would not budge. I was devastated. Wanda saw how upset I was and wanted to comfort me. She spent her own time and money to take me and Sunday to the ASPCA by taxi. At that moment, she was my big sister, and it felt good to be taken care of by her. Memories like that are the ones I try to focus on most.

For a while, Wanda went off on her own, and, as far as I could tell, she seemed to be doing well. She lived in Manhattan, which I thought was totally cool, and then later moved to California. She moved back to my folks' house in Brooklyn when I was about eighteen because I'd gotten into a car accident. (I lived.) She claimed she needed to be closer to the family during times of crisis. This made sense to me, because as dysfunctional as we were, we knew the supreme value of family.

Unfortunately, things went downhill pretty quickly for her. She spent several years on unemployment, chain-smoking, eating, and watching TV in bed. Many years later, she confided in me that she had been raped by a "friend" in California. I urged her to talk with someone about it, but she brushed it off as ancient history. Her lifestyle when she returned to New York makes sense in light of that now, but I wish she had been able to reach out for help at the time.

When my sisters decided to get an apartment together, I tried to talk them out of it to no avail. And when I visited their apartment, my worst fears were realized. It was filled with half-rotten food, ashtrays filled with cigarette butts, and decaying dog feces. I felt sad for them . . . embarrassed and concerned, but I tried to be upbeat as much as possible. Our lives were taking massively different roads, and while I truly tried to talk to them, get them motivated, and so on, my efforts sadly came to naught.

When Joanie developed early-onset Alzheimer's disease like my mom, we moved her to my dad's house in suburban New York, then later to an assisted-living facility near his home. My mother was already in a nursing home in the Bronx. On her own now, Wanda got another apartment in Brooklyn and even got a part-time job as a receptionist. I was off doing my own thing, and I was glad Wanda was working and seemed to be caring for herself.

I hadn't been to see her for the better part of a year when I finally went to visit. Walking into this apartment was like walking into a roach-infested horror movie. Rotting food was piled up near her bed, and there were bags and bags of empty unwashed soda cans and bottles she had collected from the neighbor's garbage cans. I didn't realize things had gotten this bad, and I knew it couldn't go on. I felt guilty and frustrated for not knowing how to fix my sister's life and for having left her to her own devices for too long. So, I moved her into an apartment in the area my dad and I lived. I thought that being closer to the family could help her get her life together.

By this time, my son, Dovy, was about four or five years old. Wanda simply adored him. Being closer to my home, she was able to visit with him more often, and I enjoyed watching them together. These were very sweet and precious times. Even in her confused state, she knew his value to our family.

When Wanda began roaming the streets in her nightgown late at night and taking things from stores, I realized she couldn't continue to live on her own. But I still held out hope we could find some treatment and hired a full-time aide to live with her.

I was desperate to find some explanation other than Alzheimer's disease for Wanda's confused behavior. I had already gone through this twice, with Joanie and my mom, and I had an idea of the unpleasant future that lay ahead. In spite of the odds, I contacted a local neurologist for a new workup.

Sometimes it seems you can find humor in the strangest places, and these are the memories of those days that I try to hold dear to my heart. We were at the doctor's office for the initial examination when he began testing her reasoning skills. "Wanda," he began softly, "I'm going to ask you a few questions, okay? Can you tell me, how is a banana *like* an apple?"

"I don't like apples," Wanda replied.

"That's Okay, I'm not asking whether or not you like apples, just . . . how is a banana like an apple?"

"But I don't like apples," she repeated.

He was patient with her. "My dear, Wanda, I understand you don't like apples, and we won't ask you to eat one. Just think of an apple and a banana and tell me what they have in common."

Wanda thought for a moment. She seemed to understand he would not accept her answer. Then, her eyes lit up like she suddenly got it and said, "I don't like bananas either!"

All three of us smiled. Technically, she had answered the question correctly.

It was nice to see a genuine smile on her face.

Wanda soon became incontinent and very confused, and the live-in aide said she would not be able to continue. Throughout this all, my father repeatedly offered that she come and live with him, and he would care for her. I knew that if he were to try to care for Wanda, we would quickly lose him, too.

Ultimately, we moved Wanda to a nursing facility, and although she didn't know exactly what was going on, she was very frightened by the move. I reassured her everything was fine, but as I helped her into my car, she just kept saying, "No, no, no." When she looked into my eyes, I could see how confused and scared she was. It was a hard, sorrowful day for me.

When I visit my sister, people who don't know me often ask, "Is that your mother?"

"No, my sister," I reply softly.

Wanda is now sixty-five years old. I'm certain she knows me when I visit, although she doesn't speak. I can see it in her eyes. The attendants see it, too. They all remark, "Look, she knows him, she knows him." It breaks my heart that this is something to get excited about. I never want to give up looking for something that might help my sister, but for all intents and purposes, I have.

Did Wanda catch some bad breaks in her life? Certainly she did. This is true for my mother and sister Joanie as well. Their lives were difficult, but I *know* that their illness was exacerbated by how they processed their circumstances and the events that happened to them. Did they have some disease in their body that took over? Yes. But we *all* have genetic predispositions to some infirmity or other—heart disease, diabetes, breast cancer, Alzheimer's disease. . . .

How we manage stress and our attitudes toward life can make matters worse or better. I believe we influence the physical reality in our bodies through our emotions and that the circumstances of our lives are less important than how we *perceive* and define them. Emotions of fear and hate and worry and guilt release toxins; they can make us sick. Emotions of love and hope and joy release healing agents; they can strengthen our immune system and our body's defenses. We don't always have control over events in our lives, but we can control our own reactions and responses. Attitude and perception are everything and joy promotes health.

Does that mean that positive, loving people will never get sick? If we could totally control our brain, the answer would be yes. But few, if any, have that power. Yet we can take hold of our attitudes and perceptions every day. Our birthright is to live in hope and joy, in love and gratitude. We just have to choose to grab on to it.

I don't blame my sister. I love her with all my heart and wish she had been able to find a path to live in joy and love. And I try to use her experience, and that of my sister Joanie, and my mom, to remind myself that I need to live in the light. That if I become too stressed, or anxious, or fearful, that I, too, could fall ill and jeopardize all that

I hold dear. Lives like my sisters need not be as sad as they appear if they help others to learn. And Wanda is still alive and young—who knows what the future holds.

DRUGS
(or Having a "Good" Time While You Play)

"I said to a guy, 'Tell me, what is it about cocaine
that makes it so wonderful,' and he said,
'Well, it intensifies your personality.'
I said, 'Yes, but what if you're an asshole?'"

—Bill Cosby

THERE'S A GOOD REASON that the triumvirate of sex, drugs, and rock-'n'-roll has become part of the vernacular. They often play a role in a young person's journey to find their way—and they certainly did for me. The convergence of these three, combined with a young man's search for himself, led me far away from that little boy in Brooklyn—almost too far away from home to return.

When I was growing up, my parents never thought of warning me about the dangers of doing drugs—not that I would have listened. We didn't really connect in that way. It was almost as if we lived in different worlds by the time I reached high school. In fact, when my father finally tried to give me my first "sex" talk, I gently let him off the hook. I probably knew more than him.

Surprisingly, my early years as a musician did not expose me to drugs or alcohol too much. While I did some drugs in high school to be cool and fit in, I wasn't faced with the ultimate test until I went off to college.

I was accepted to the State University at Stonybrook. Although it was a very good school academically, it had a reputation for being a "drug school." I barely attended high school in my senior year, so I was thrilled to be accepted, and so were my parents. My school almost didn't even let me graduate on time because of my attendance, but I got the ACLU to threaten to sue if they didn't. Hey, I was a middle-class Jewish kid—I was definitely going to a good college, high school or no high school.

I quickly befriended a wild crowd that was doing that out-of-control-kids-at-college thing, and we experimented with various drugs. It all seemed perfectly natural to me. I already knew some of these kids from high school, and none of us were the studious type.

One night after doing a combination of organic mescaline and cocaine along with the usual booze and pot, I flipped out. My worst fears had come true when my roommate told me to go the bathroom and check out my penis. I did—and to my everlasting horror—it wasn't there. It had totally receded into my body—or at least that's what I thought. Who knows what's real when you're tripping. But I'm pretty sure it was mostly gone—like much worse than swimming-in-cold-water gone (*"It shrinks?"*).

My friends tried to talk me down by telling me that's what normally happens when you mix coke and mescaline, but I wasn't buying any of it. My penis was *my life*, and seeing it gone was simply too much to handle. Soon enough, my heart starting racing, and I thought for sure I was having a heart attack. I finally fell asleep (or maybe my friends just knocked me out since I was ruining their trips), and in truth, I was fine in the morning, a little freaked out, but fine. A good time was had by all.

Every addict has their drug of choice, or should I say, drug of weakness. For some it's alcohol or tobacco or uppers/downers or heroine or marijuana. (One of my friends used to say he'd been smoking pot for forty years and never got hooked.) I didn't have a problem with any of those drugs. My drug of weakness was cocaine.

Good cocaine convinced me that I was on top of the world—the euphoric kind of mood, where nothing could possibly be wrong or confusing or bad. My friends and I would get into really cool "coke raps," and as we talked about how much we loved each other (*"I really love you, man"*), we'd swear it wasn't a coke rap. Coke wasn't a lethargy-inducing drug; it just made the user feel *good*, and because that feeling was so fleeting and short lived, the only thing to bring it back was . . . more coke. And this stuff wasn't cheap.

My friends and I were doing so much blow, it just made financial sense to buy a bunch, sell some, keep some for "the head," and use the profits to buy some more. We were totally out of control; the cocaine was pretty much running (or should I say, ruining?) our lives. Going to class became an occasional pastime. We managed to get by for a while acting like complete morons and doing dangerous things, but it soon caught up with us. We were attracting too much unwanted attention, which culminated in a friend of ours being killed by a drug supplier as a signal for us to cool it.

Seeing death so up close like that and facing the hard reality of losing a friend got me to wise up. But only just a bit. I left college for a road gig, and that saved me from getting in deeper, at least at school, where it seemed my life was actually in jeopardy. I was nineteen years old.

Contrary to my earlier experience as a musician, it became clear to me on the road that many musicians did drugs and drank a lot of alcohol, so I joined in by smoking pot and drinking, too. In fact, one night during the big "streaking" craze of the 1970s, I was so high I ran stone-cold naked across the bar in the Terre Haute, Indiana, Ramada Inn where we were playing. I'm lucky no one ratted on me, because the troopers were there in no time. When the tour ended, I made a failed attempt to continue my college education. I just couldn't get into all the rules, and so, I struck out in the world as a full-time musician.

I performed at every kind of gig imaginable, and although I did coke every now and then, I was able to keep my use in check (if drug use can ever be kept in check) by periodically getting way over my head into debt.

My cocaine problem and I didn't seriously meet up again until I landed a gig at the Red Parrot Nightclub in New York City when I was in my late twenties. This place was a new trendy nightclub that opened up on the West Side of Manhattan as the new entry to the ultra-hip club world that arose after Studio 54. It was the kind of place where people would stand in line to get in, and fat-headed bouncers with more muscle than brains would decide which of the beautiful people to let in. I hated that part.

The idea of the club was unique. It featured an eighteen-piece swing band, made up of all the best players in town, who traded off sets with a name club DJ. The club opened at 11:30 PM, and the band would never start before midnight. I was able to play a Broadway show a few blocks away and still make it to the gig with plenty of time to spare. We would work until about 4 AM and then go in search of an after-hours club! Actually, most of the time, I would head to the only sushi place in town that was still open at that time—Chin Ya in the Woodward Hotel. (In a crazy coincidence, I later found out that my wife, Lisa, had frequented the same place at the same time in her "crazy" days.)

I met everyone from Mick Jagger to Sylvester Stallone at the Red Parrot, and performed with people like Cab Calloway and Whitney Houston. I was a little celebrity in my own right and had all the perks to go along with it, including the Penthouse Pet of the Month. And there were drugs . . . lots of drugs. You could never take a dump at this place because all the bathroom stalls were full of people doing blow. Everyone wanted to turn me on, so for the year I worked there it seemed money would not be the deciding factor in stopping my drug use. *There would be no one to save the princess this time.*

I spent my evenings at the Red Parrot high on cocaine and Cristal Champagne, until one night when it all came crashing down, and the reality of what I was doing slapped me right in the face.

I was the drummer in the band with a feature drum solo each night, but I was also the male singer. Another drummer played when I went to the front of the stage for my vocal numbers. The night in question, I was so high that I barely made it back to the bandstand to relieve the DJ after our break. I had done so much blow that my heart felt like it was exploding out of my chest, and I actually felt like I could die right then and there.

I'd barely made it to the drums when the bandleader signaled for me to come up front and sing one of my numbers. My breath came out in short gasps and my legs felt like Jell-O, but I somehow managed to make my way to the front. The eighteen-piece band went into the intro for my number. It all felt so surreal, and I panicked. I knew my vocal cords wouldn't work—I could barely breathe, much less sing. If I even tried to get a note out, it would be clear to everyone that I was blasted, and I'd lose all credibility as well as my job. So when the time came for me to sing, I just mouthed a few of the words. I shook my fist at the soundman to imply that the mic wasn't working, and since we always had trouble with the sound, the bandleader bought it. I tossed the mic down in feigned disgust and crawled my way back to the drums.

While this wasn't the traditional "I hit bottom and lost everything" story, my drug use completely ended that night. I truly felt that close to death, and it scared the hell out of me. I'd already seen two friends die from drug overdose, and I didn't intend to join them. With all the death in my family's history, I knew that life was far too precious to waste it that way. Sure, I was into having a good time, but I was never so stupid or out of control that I would knowingly risk my life. I was only so stupid and out of control enough to risk it *unknowingly*.

The next evening, I took all my drug paraphernalia to the club— my coke vials, my gold coke spoons and necklaces, and anything else I had that was related to drugs—and I gave them all away to my drug friends who usually turned me on. Stopping cold turkey was challenging at first in the face of my friends who were using, but ultimately, I was that nice Jewish kid from Brooklyn my parents thought I was, and this was not the direction I would allow my life to take. I wisely put some distance between myself and my drug friends and managed to avoid the temptation. (A year or two later, I did a line of coke at a party just out of curiosity to see what would happen—one sniff and I rushed off to the bathroom to vomit. Good deal.)

It wasn't as if I hadn't seen the real dangers of drug use before this experience. The owner of the musician-occupied bungalow colony where I lived (and met my thirty year old girlfriend) for a time died that summer from an overdose. Harry was a young, beautiful trumpet player who had worked with Art Blakey and other jazz greats, and he left behind a loving wife and brother. He had seemingly kicked his habit, but went back for one more thrill. He'd once told me jazz was "having a good time when you played." Harry taught me not to overthink things and to try to be in the moment so you can be free. Now, I try to incorporate that into all my performances, and I thank Harry for that bit of wisdom. His loss was senseless.

Some years ago, my dad and I were watching a PBS documentary about drug use.

"Why would anyone do such a thing?" he wondered aloud.

I replied, "Out of curiosity."

He turned to me and gave me a deep, searching look. "It sounds like you may have tried it," he said.

I looked him squarely in the eye. "Dad, let's get it all on the table. Anything you think I may have done, let's just assume I did it."

The hurt expression on his face spoke volumes, but all he said was "I'm very disappointed."

"Dad, I don't do it any longer," I said. "Be proud of me. I fought my demons off, and I'm still here."

Barely. I was lucky to survive my excesses, and I've come out a stronger person for it, but I might easily have been a sad statistic. The list of my other friends who were not as lucky has continued to grow over the years. I've experienced gambling, womanizing, drug use, overeating, and excesses of every sort, and the feeling is always the same—not enough. It never feels like there is enough—you always want more. I've learned that the "more" I was looking for doesn't come from any of those things. And I've learned many other lessons from my excesses, and I've become a wiser person for it.

However, I'm hoping my son can learn his lessons a different way. I speak with Dovy about the dangers of doing drugs or drinking when it comes up naturally, although he's only eleven. Ironically, the abundance of drug commercials on TV gives me a great opening to discuss the problem of reaching for drugs (both legal and illegal) to cure our ills, instead of trying to work through them. The danger inherent in taking drugs couldn't be more clearly illustrated than by just listening to the list of potential side effects at the end of the commercial. Dovy and I actually have a good laugh over our favorite side effect: death. Another top-ten favorite is "call your doctor if you have increased thoughts of suicide" following an ad for an antidepressant. And we make up funny ones: "If your eye falls out and your right ear explodes, call your doctor as this may be the sign of a rare but serious condition." It would be truly funny if it weren't so sad.

Our culture is full of the notion that salvation comes from a pill. Why should we be surprised when kids abuse drugs? We're busy telling them that answers come from outside of themselves—not from searching within. I tell my son that drugs are a waste of time, that they prevent you from becoming your best self, that they're dangerous, and that being out of control doesn't feel good. My wife and I try to give him the best tools we can to help him make good decisions when Mommy and Daddy aren't around—like when he's sixteen or seventeen and he's exposed to new, potentially dangerous, choices. No matter how hard we try to protect him from this, he will undoubtedly be faced with this decision. I wonder how I would feel hearing from him what my father had to hear from me. I hope I never find out.

And I hope he's smart enough to avoid testing each of the waters I tested, to see if the answers are there. As for me, my personal journey would continue. . . .

TANTE REGINA

(or Someone Not to Be Trifled With)

"It's a wonder I haven't abandoned all my ideals,
they seem so absurd and impractical.
Yet I cling to them because I still believe, in spite of
everything, that people are truly good at heart."
—Anne Frank

I'VE ALWAYS BEEN ACUTELY AWARE of the tenuous nature of civilization, and the fragile structure of society that keeps us together. I'm certain that is a direct result of having grown up in a family whose lives were shattered through the total breakdown of everything civilized we live by. I didn't focus on that in my life, and in fact, most of the time I avoided it—as did my father. But there was no avoiding the internal awareness—even when unspoken—of what we were the surviving remnants of. Yet, in the process of protecting ourselves from this trauma, many things were hidden, and much passed out of our awareness. My closest link to my extended family, and the life they knew before the Shoah (Holocaust) was my grandfather's sister—my father's aunt—and my great aunt, "Tante" Regina.

My tante Regina was the oldest surviving member of my family and the nearest thing I had to a grandmother. She came to the United States by way of France in 1949. Like the rest of the members of my parents' families along with countless others, the course of Tante

Regina's life was drastically altered because of the Holocaust.

Some of the few items my tante Regina still had in her possession from her life in Europe are now in my care. I recently took one of these items to an antique road-show type of event that was taking place at the Gomez Mill House—the oldest Jewish-occupied dwelling in North America dating back to the early 1700s. There would be a few antique appraisers there, and I thought it would be interesting to share my aunt's items for appraisal. The items I chose to bring were two glass urns (or jugs) housed in their own custom-made case. I had a vague sense of the urns' history, and although they originally had a letter of authentication with them, the document became lost over time.

The antique appraisers were kind and friendly folk, and the atmosphere was very informal. I arrived late in the afternoon, just as the show was winding down. Many people at the event knew me and had known my dad. There was some lighthearted banter about what I might be hiding in this strange locked case.

The appraisers joined in the fun, saying, "Okay! Let's see what *treasure* you've got here."

I could have told them what I knew about the items, but I didn't want to sway them, so I said nothing as I opened the case. Immediately, the joking died down and the appraisers fell silent. They were dumbstruck. The onlookers fell silent as well in reaction to the expressions on the appraisers' faces.

After a few moments, one appraiser finally said, "Oh my goodness, these are magnificent!" She carefully lifted one out of the case. "These are certainly not American. They're handmade from somewhere in Europe, probably France."

She met my eyes with intention and continued, "An average person doesn't have a possession like this. There are not a dozen of these in the world, there are not three, there is only one. This is a possession that would belong to a king or a queen."

The other appraisers chimed in and their praise of the urns went on for some time. They thanked me over and over for making their day by bringing in such a rare and unique heirloom for them to see. They implored me to go to one of the big auction houses like Sotheby's to get the urns properly appraised. They were sure the value would be enormous.

I was not as taken aback as those around me. I knew the stories about my tante Regina—and my father's family in general—before the war in Poland. But I was glad to have the reaction to the urns corroborate what little I knew.

My tante Regina was one of seven children, including my grandfather Yankel, after whom I am named. My dad always used to say that the Ehrenreichs were people of extremes—either huge successes or huge failures, nothing in between. Interestingly, by contrast my father was a person who prided himself in moderation—I guess we all rebel against our parents. My tante Regina was one of the successes, at least financially.

I first started to truly understand this when I received a phone call from my tante in Philadelphia when I was living in Manhattan. I was probably in my twenties at the time.

She said she needed to speak to me. When I told her I was listening, she said no, I needed to go to Philadelphia so she could speak to me in person. My tante could be quite forceful and demanding like that, although she was very diminutive in size. She was a little old lady living in a small apartment on the outskirts of Philadelphia, but she sometimes behaved as though she were of royal blood.

"Tante, it's a far drive to Philadelphia, can't you at least tell me what it's about?" I pleaded.

"Vy do you esk qvestions? If I say you hev to come to Philadelphia, you hev to come to Philadelphia!" she demanded. She was tough and not one to be trifled with.

I arrived in Philly later that week on a rainy afternoon. She made cream-cheese sandwiches for us, and while we ate, we caught up on the everyday things we'd been doing. When we were done, she made her way to the hallway closet, opened it, and pointed to a large cardboard box way up on top: "There, take that down."

I placed the box on the floor, and, as she pointed to it, she said, "That's it, you have to take care of this."

Take care of what? I thought. I opened the box to find it filled with letters in French, Polish, and Yiddish from the 1940s up to the 1960s . . . every language but English. She proceeded to explain that our family had owned a spectacular villa in Nice, France, in the finest section. It was still there, and the entire matter had never been addressed. She had decided that I should be the one to solve this.

I took this all with a grain of salt. Although I had heard rumors of my tante's having been some sort of big deal in Europe before the war, all I saw in front of me was a little old lady who can best be described as bearing a striking resemblance to Yoda from *Star Wars*. She was maybe four feet tall and had that look that old ladies get when they finally become gender neutral—she wore a kerchief on her head from which her ears stuck out on either side, and her age was indeterminate. I took the box and left with the promise that I would find out what I could.

I called my dad when I got back to New York and told him what had transpired in Philadelphia. He was very dismissive. "She's a crazy old lady, why are you listening to her?" he said.

I thought about this for a few days. I didn't want to hurt my tante's feelings, but I didn't want to waste my time either. I decided to call Tante Regina and tell her what my dad had said.

She became incensed. "Your *father*?! Your *father*?!" she repeated, clearly astonished. "You asked your *father*? What does *he* know? He was just a *baby*! Why do ask your father? He doesn't know *anything*!" She continued to ream me out for a while, and when she was done, I apologized and assured her I'd take care of the matter. It was weird to hear my father described as being *"just a baby"* who knew nothing—it got me thinking about the bigger picture, and how little I really knew about our family history.

Notwithstanding what my father had said, something in my tante's fury had a convincing ring of sincerity. Also, I knew my father had put many details of the life he had lived before the war behind him. It would make sense that he would naturally want to let sleeping dogs lie—if he, in fact, knew anything at all. I decided to take this matter a bit further. I took several letters that looked important, and simply wrote the following letter to the addresses on the envelopes.

"My name is Jacob Isaac Ehrenreich. I am the grand nephew of Maria Regina Swerdlik née Ehrenreich. Your address was found in some correspondence relating to 'La Villa Noria' in Nice, France. Any information you can provide to me would be greatly appreciated."

Some letters came back undeliverable; some not at all. I got a response from someone who said I must be looking for his father of the same name, but he had passed some years ago. However, one letter contained an offer to buy our share of the property.

I was stunned. This confirmed the feeling I had and the ring of truth I heard when speaking with Tante Regina. I began to clearly realize for the first time how much family historical information is lost in just a generation or two.

The story of this property is long and complicated. Suffice it to say for now that I visited the property in Nice, which was at the time, about four acres of land in the finest area, overlooking the city. There was an abandoned villa on the property. Vagrants were squatting there; there had been a murder. I spent some time meeting with lawyers and the real estate company that now controlled the property for the unknown heirs like me. Ultimately, the red tape proved too much for me at the time, and I put it on the back burner. All things that have to with my family who existed before the war are shrouded in shadow and bring up feelings that are hard to decipher. It's a place that can prevent me from living in the present if I let it.

I told my tante Regina I'd keep working on it, but I haven't really. The disposition of this property is still unresolved. Perhaps someday I'll pick up the thread again.

Many years after Tante Regina's death, I had the opportunity to go to Poland to make a documentary about current Jewish life there—or more precisely, what was left of it. On the trip, I decided to visit my dad's childhood home and other family sites, including my tante Regina's hometown. My trip to Poland brought to light even more details about the life my tante Regina had led there, and some pieces to the puzzle of who she was started making sense.

But my first order of business was to search out where my father had lived as a child. This was proving to be more difficult than I had imagined and was causing some strife between me and my guide—which was unusual, because I really liked him. My dad had told me his farm was on "Gosciniec Road," and I passed along this information—but in all the times I heard him ask for directions, I never once heard him say, "Gosciniec Road," despite my constant reminders. To be honest, I was getting pretty frustrated and pissed off, and I finally told him so. My guide turned to me and said, "Look, 'gosciniec road' just means 'dirt road' in Polish." My face flushed. We'd only finally found my dad's home when he started asking where the *Zhyd* (Jew) had lived. Then people immediately knew—they got very animated and said repeatedly *"Zhyd! Zhyd!"* as if to say, *"Why didn't you say so in the first place? . . . the Jew lived over there."*

We were way out in the countryside, and although I never asked, I later figured perhaps my guide thought it better to be a little more low key.

We were in a little town called Zakshuv—my father's family was very wealthy when he was young, and they had a farming estate there. His family was very orthodox and followed the Ger Rebbe of the Hassidic movement. Hassidism was a branch of Orthodox Judaism that promoted spirituality and joy as the fundamental aspects of Jewish faith. My father later became secular and developed major disagreements with Hassidism and orthodoxy in general, but he never forgot the very deep traditional education of his youth.

In the early years, my father's family had a tutor who lived with them and taught my father and his siblings. I pictured them huddled by the fire in the winter learning their lessons. It reminded me of the Yiddish song *"Oyfn Pripetchik"* (by the fireplace), which speaks of the same scene. He loved those days growing up on the farm, and I know it always influenced his desire to live in the country, which he eventually did.

When we finally found the farm where my dad grew up, the house seemed nothing like what I had pictured; it was much smaller. Maybe there had been another structure there before that had been torn down. The family living there was very welcoming and kind. I made clear we were not there to try to reclaim anything—my family had sold this property years before the war. As it turned out, they knew nothing of my family. They had only recently purchased the property themselves. But they believed the neighbor had been living there since before the war; perhaps she knew something. They brought us over to their yard. At the mere mention of my grandfather's name "Yankel," the woman began to scream and run away. *"Yankel! Yankel!"* She disappeared from sight and did not return while we were there. I'll never know what that was all about, but it made me recall the story of my mom's uncle who had been shot and killed by locals after the war when he went to reclaim his home. I was slowly coming to realize that for Jews, Poland was a land full of ghosts.

Next, I was scheduled to go to Prushkov, where my tante Regina had lived. Because she'd since passed on, I had only my dad to rely on for directions. I called him trans-Atlantically (which was a bigger deal in those days than it is today) to get whatever information he could provide to help us find the place. The whole dirt road business was fresh in my mind, so I had a fairly dim opinion of his knowledge in these matters. In his defense, Tante Regina had said, "He was just a baby." *So, why was I asking him?* Because he was all I had.

Surprisingly, his directions were very specific: "Go to Prushkov and ask around." That was my father's brilliant advice for finding a house that my great-aunt lived in fifty years earlier. After my last episode, I was not in the mood for ridiculous directions from my father yet again. We began arguing at long-distance intercontinental phone rates. He wouldn't budge.

"Go to Prushkov," he demanded. "Say the name Ehrenreich. If they don't know it, then it's gone."

The next morning, I relayed this GPS-like information to my guide. Allow me to describe his reaction in Yiddish-flavored English—*happy, he wasn't.*

"Prushkov is a city of fifty thousand people!" he exclaimed. "Are you kidding?"

I sheepishly said, "It's the best I can do, let's just go."

"It's your money," he replied.

A few hours later, when we arrived in the city of Prushkov, it was late afternoon. "Here we are, Prushkov," he said. "Would you like me to stop and ask that lady on the street?" he asked facetiously.

I had a thought. "Hey, isn't there some kind of town hall or museum or something where we could get some information?"

As it turns out, there was a museum just a few blocks away. When we got there, my driver approached the visitor's desk at the museum and, with embarrassment written all over his face, spoke a few words in Polish to the female attendant. The only thing I could make out was "Ehrenreich."

With surprise evident in her tone, she asked, "Ehrenreich?"

My guide pointed at me, and she motioned for him to wait. She scurried off and when she returned, she was followed by the director of the museum. The director spoke with my guide, whose eyes widened. As the conversation died down, they seemed to come to some sort of agreement. The director firmly shook my hand, said something I couldn't understand, then left.

My guide turned to me with somewhat of a grin on his face and said, "This museum was your tante Regina's house. The porcelain factory across the street, which belonged to your family and was run by your great-aunt was, and still is, one of the largest in Poland. You have a tour of the factory at six tomorrow morning."

I was stunned by this news, and very, very excited. I had an unusual feeling I'd never felt before, similar yet different from what I'd felt at my father's house. It was confusing and exhilarating, and a bit frightening—like a door was opening to a past I'd only heard whispers of. I felt as if I were entering a royal world full of lost bones and secrets long buried. I was silent on the drive all the way back to Warsaw.

The next morning, I felt like a celebrity on par with Michael Jackson. The head of the factory and several scientists took me on a tour of the porcelain factory, showing me the ins and outs of the new furnaces they had installed. I nodded, as if I knew anything about porcelain making.

My arrival must have been announced, because later that morning, I noticed a freshly drawn "JUDE" (Jew) with a Star of David on one of the dusty windows—that's just how the Nazis used to identify Jewish businesses in the early days. By now, I was getting less and less surprised by the very odd relationship between the Poles and the Jews, and the unmistakable vibe that there was old, unfinished business here. During one of our interviews for the documentary, a young local reporter told us the hippest thing with young Poles was to find out if you had any Jewish blood in your family. I was shocked. And we visited a Jewish center where an American rabbi was counseling young Poles who had recently found out they were, in fact, Jewish, but that information had been hidden from them. And there were non-Jewish Poles trying to save Jewish cemeteries—and people spoke of the huge hole that had been left in Polish society by the destruction of millions of its citizens—a full 10 percent of the population. And there was still anti-Semitism—but not as active, because after a thousand years of Jewish life in Poland, there were no longer enough Jews to hate.

At the end of the tour of my family's factory, there was some discussion by the factory principals about the fact that whatever had "belonged" to my family had already been distributed to a relative from England. This had become a theme in Poland: everyone seemed afraid that any Jews returning to Poland would try to reclaim their family property.

I made it clear that I was not there to try to reclaim anything—that was not the purpose of my visit, and that put them somewhat at ease. On our way back to my great-aunt's "house," the museum director told me what he knew of her. He spoke of a very close relationship with the president of Poland and intimated there may have been a romance between them, but that was second- or thirdhand information. This was getting stranger by the minute. I saw historical plates in the museum with my family name on it. I was astonished and confused—I'd known nothing of this.

Most of the time, I didn't know exactly what to do with this information or how to deal with my feelings, so I kept them in. I felt emotionally lost. My family seemed so distant to me—like a dream out of someone else's life. I was angry that the opportunity to know them had been taken from me—but it was a little late to be angry now. Photos of my great-aunt lounging in front of this enormous mansion reinforced the scene in my mind. I pictured her youngest brother Janek—who survived the war, and I had met—driving around in his first Lancia car in Europe. But I couldn't picture my grandfather, because I had never seen even a photograph of him.

As I thought about my tante Regina, her personality started to make more sense to me. She had been accustomed to a life none of us ever quite understood or wanted to know about.

I have an audiotape from some years back in which my aunt is being interviewed about her life during the war. During the interview, my tante Regina said, *"Di beste mentshn zenen imgekimen."* (The best of us did not survive.)

That thought—that the best perished—has remained with me all these years and always will. It is a common theme among survivors, and the guilt often associated with survivors of the Holocaust is clearly evident in that phrase. Yet, I think it was also Tante's attempt to pay homage to those heroes of whom we now know nothing, mostly Jews, but non Jews as well. Certainly many wonderful people survived, but many of the best were lost and their stories with them.

Tante Regina married but never had children. She settled in Philadelphia with her husband, Oscar Swerdlik, who passed fairly young, and she lived alone for many years. We offered several times for her to come live with my dad, but she always refused. The time finally came when she was just getting too old to live on her own. She was stubborn and willful, but I had to try. She said she could not come to live with my dad because he had a dog—and she simply could not live with a dog. After much wrangling, we settled on a "compromise"—I would move her to my dad's in New York, and if she didn't like the dog, or anything about the move, I would move her back to Philadelphia. Moving my aunt twice was my worst nightmare, but that's how one had to deal with Tante Regina.

After four hours of being reprimanded for driving too fast, I finally loaded her into my dad's house in Upstate New York and escaped back to Manhattan. A few days went by, and I heard no complaints about the dog. So far so good. A couple of weeks later, I went up for dinner. Again, there was no mention of the dog, and, as a matter of fact, my aunt and Hintl (which means "small dog" in Yiddish) seemed pretty chummy. I was surprised and ecstatic. During dessert, I turned to Tante Regina and said, "So, Tante, what do you know? It's not so bad living with a dog, huh?"

"No!" she said emphatically, ruffling Hintl's furry head. "This is not a dog. This is a mentsh!" (An upstanding person.)

That's what I loved about Tante Regina; she was one of those people you just couldn't argue with. I found it funny and entertaining, and I loved her for it.

In fact, my visits to my dad over the years when Tante lived with him were always filled with quirky and entertaining adventures. One visit took place on a scorchingly hot summer day. My dad had an air conditioner in the living room, but for him to actually turn it on, I think the sun would have to go supernova. My sisters and I were sitting on the couch—or should I more accurately say, we were stuck to the forty-year-old yellowing, cracked plastic slipcovers "protecting" the still-pristine couch. That couch was older than I was, and in perfect condition. We were all wearing shorts of course, and our flesh was adhered to the plastic. I almost ripped off half my thigh trying to get up to use the toilet. *Who invented these things, the Marquis de Sade?* They are like condoms for furniture. Did they think a chair and sofa would get together at night and make an ottoman? (Hey, maybe that's why they call it a loveseat.)

My sisters and I decided enough was enough. We peeled ourselves off the couch and began removing the ancient slipcovers.

"Vhat are you doing?" Tante Regina shouted and started freaking out like an addict in withdrawal, yelling and flailing her arms. Yup, she was clearly hooked on the plastic—this was like taking a needle from a junky. My father told us to just forget about it and leave it alone, but he didn't really care one way or the other. But Wanda, Joanie, and I were on the quest for the holy grail of plastic-free fabric to sit on. We would finally rid ourselves of the instrument of torture, which had inflicted decades of misery on us and on many more like us or we would go down trying. We had seen the enemy—and he was us (just older).

Once the slipcovers had been removed and Tante Regina had finally calmed down, my sisters and I headed home. A few weeks later, I visited again. I simply shook my head when I saw what Tante Regina had done: she had completely covered the living room furniture with towels, dishcloths, sheets, and other *shmattas*. My Yoda aunt simply would not be defeated. The force was strong with her.

Stubbornness was Tante's forte. I needed to fill in her birthdate on a form, and when I asked for it, she replied emphatically, "A voman doesn't tell her age." I just stared at her dumbfounded. I felt like saying, "Your age? I can't tell your gender!" but of course I held my tongue.

We never did find out how old she was. But thirty-nine, she wasn't. In later years, she was in and out of the hospital. At one visit, her prognosis seemed quite bleak. Her doctor approached my dad and asked if we had instructions for her final care. Since we did not, he told us to find out from her what her wishes were. I volunteered to do it and entered the room alone.

My tante looked like she was almost gone. This made me sad, but not overly so—she had lived a long life and had experienced some joy, and she was not alone at the end. I sat close to her bed and spoke softly and kindly. We spoke in Yiddish.

"Tante," I said. "You know you're ill. We are sure you will get better, but the doctors need to know now about your personal wishes, just in case. If things got very bad, would you want to pass peacefully and naturally and quietly . . . or would you want to be hooked up to all sorts of machines?"

Her eyes popped open with life, and she said, "Are you crazy? Hook me up to everything!"

I smiled. Maybe the prognosis wasn't so bad after all. And, in fact, she recovered and to everyone's astonishment, lived many more years.

My tante Regina was a holdover from a time gone by and the last living remnant of what the Ehrenreich family had been. I can still see her sitting on the couch near my father while he gave his testimony for Steven Spielberg's Shoah Foundation, but she never had the opportunity to fully tell her own incredible story. I should have tried harder to get more stories from her, and I regret that I didn't. If you take anything away from this essay, I hope it is this: Ask the older folks in your family about their lives before it's too late. You're entitled to know as much as they can tell you. It's your history, too.

I never knew any grandparents. Tante Regina was the closest thing I had to that sort of relationship, and I loved her dearly. After she was gone, I finally wised up and began asking my dad for more information about what he remembered of his family's life. That was great, but what did he know anyway? He was just a baby.

ROCK-'N'-ROLL
(or The All-American Gig)

"Music is your own experience,
your own thoughts, your own wisdom.
If you don't live it, it won't come out of your horn."
—Charlie Parker

MY TWENTIES WERE PROBABLY my wildest years. I think this was actually fairly common for kids born anytime in the 1950s—although my carousing continued into my early thirties. These were formative, searching, crazy years, and I tried everything. I was fortunate to have music to make money, to give me unique traveling experiences, and to basically allow me to live the lifestyle I'd always wanted while I searched for meaning. I wasn't in close contact with my family during this time, although we were never estranged. I was just off doing my own thing, and living my rock-'n'-roll American dream. It was important for me to make that break, and I did. I was fitting in well now, and I was pretty fearless. I hadn't been called Yonkee in a very long time. I never in my wildest dreams imagined I'd end up caring for my entire family a few years later.

From the time my mother sang to me as an infant, I was in love with music . . . all music. But as a kid, to me, rock-'n'-roll music was synonymous with everything about being a "real" American. Listening to it on my transistor radio and knowing the groups of the day made me feel like I fit in. Rock music even got intertwined in my mind with Christmas music, which dominated the airwaves for a few weeks every year. It all seemed so legitimately American, everything I wanted to be and everything my Jewish immigrant family was not. I got a real shocker later in life when I found out how many of the rock songs I loved were actually written by Jews. Especially the Christmas songs!

But when I talk about rock-'n'-roll here, it's not only about the music. Rock-'n'-roll is a lifestyle and an attitude, as well as a style of music. "Let's rock-'n'-roll" means much more than let's play some of that rock-'n'-roll music. You play music—you *live* rock-'n'-roll.

I happily and successfully lived the rock-'n'-roll "lifestyle" for many years, and I even had a couple of close calls with actually becoming a rock star, too. I recorded with Richie Havens and auditioned with Edgar Winter, but the closest I ever came was when I auditioned for KISS in 1982 after drummer Peter Criss left the band. I was not a KISS fan by any stretch, but I would have taken the gig in a heartbeat—just for the lifestyle. I was so close to getting the gig that I played with the band in a rehearsal hall in New York City. I was disappointed I didn't ultimately get it, but it was actually fun to play a bunch of their tunes, and even sing a few. Maybe I should have sung in Yiddish! That's a joke, but in an odd twist I didn't know at the time, both Gene Simmons and Paul Stanley of KISS are children of Holocaust survivors. It would have been some trip if I had actually gotten the gig.

I was probably fortunate not to have landed the KISS gig—or one like it—who knows where my out-of-control drug use might have led me in that environment. But it was never really my passion to be a big rock star. I was just out for some fun, and I had some, too. One of my favorite nights was when I got to play drums with Greg Allman of the Allman Brothers Band at the Lone Star Roadhouse in Manhattan. It was really cool to play Allman Brothers tunes I had listened to in college, with one of the *real* Allman brothers. I had the time of my life, but I think the best part of that night actually happened the following day. I was walking on West Broadway near my Soho apartment, with a new date I was trying hard to impress. A couple of really cute chicks came toward us, and as they came closer, one came directly up to me. "Excuse me. Weren't you playing drums with Greg Allman at the Lone Star Roadhouse last night?" I wish I could have bottled that moment. *Point, set, match. Game over.*

I was pretty much a musician-for-hire from an early age, and in that capacity, I worked a lot as a hired gun with all types of artists and bands. In a way the closest I got to experience what it felt like to be a full-fledged rock star was as Ringo Starr in the New Zealand tour of Beatlemania. The Beatles had toured New Zealand in the early years during the real Beatle craze, and we simply followed in their footsteps many years later. When we arrived in a city, the front page of the local newspaper would feature an original photo of the Beatles, alongside a photo of us in the same pose at the same location. Even the photo shoots themselves were a scene as they got leaked to local Beatle fan clubs. We were as close as an eighteen-year-old coed was ever likely to get to a real Beatle.

The Beatlemania guys were always giving me a hard time (for giving them a hard time). For instance, we took a press photo at a crosswalk that mimicked the Abbey Road album cover. The guys couldn't wait to see the photo. However, upon viewing it, the band let out a collective moan of disapproval . . . directed at me.

"What?" I asked innocently.

"Don't you know only Paul has his right foot forward? You messed up the whole shot!"

It was the whole Paul-is-dead thing. Hey, nobody told *me*. The other guys in the band were really into every facet of Beatle trivia. The guy playing John almost knocked me off my drum seat during a performance when he shouted, "Stop the war!" into the mic at full volume during "Come Together." When I asked him what the heck that was, he was mortified to learn that I didn't know that in some stadium concert in 1970-whatever, John Lennon shouted that phrase at exactly that point of that tune. *Hmmmm.*

I liked the Beatles as much as anyone else, but it was a gig to me. All the other Beatlemania guys had gone to "Beatle school" for many months to learn how to look and sound like the original Beatles. I learned the show in a week of studying tapes and video. I took pride in doing a great job, and I enjoyed the challenge and the music, but I didn't feel as though I needed to become a Beatle savant. In fact, dissecting Ringo's drum parts note for note actually took away some of the magic and mystery that Beatle's music held for me as a child. But I also learned something about the difference between music and virtuosity. I had always thought Ringo was a mediocre drummer. When I actually started to understand the nuances of his playing on a deeper level, I saw that his unique style of playing perfectly supported the Beatles brilliant and revolutionary music. He may not have been a virtuoso, but he was a great musician.

The gig was paying great money, so I had the freedom not to stay with the rest of the band in whatever fancy hotel they were staying at.

I rented a motorcycle for the whole tour and I'd search out unusual, out-of-the-way places in each city and stay there. *Very* rock-'n'-roll of me, I thought—and in fact, this led to some interesting and unusual experiences.

Since I was playing the rock-star thing for all it was worth, I decided to rent the honeymoon suite in a charming little inn I'd found at the outskirts of Wanganui. (I love the name of that city. It's pronounced *wan-ga-noo-ee*. It sounds like an infielder for the Pittsburgh Pirates. *Now batting . . . playing second base . . . number 12 . . . Juan Ganui.*) It was a truly unique and beautiful suite, complete with red-velvet drapes and a gorgeous gold harp located on a stand in the middle of the living room. It was extremely romantic—right out of the middle ages, and I was making pretty good use of it, too.

One day the proprietor asked if a production company might have access to the suite for an hour or two the next morning. They had begun a photo shoot there before I arrived, and as it turns out, they needed to get just a few more shots. I said I planned to be in the next morning—it was okay with me if they came around eleven.

The next morning I was in my robe making toast and eggs when a young guy and a girl arrived, carrying equipment for the shoot. As was my style in those days, I immediately noticed how much of a knockout the gal was. They set up the lights and whatever else they needed, then asked my permission to start the shoot. I told them not to mind me—just pretend as if I wasn't there. To my everlasting surprise, this strikingly beautiful twenty-year-old took off her blouse and skirt to reveal the sexiest undergarments I'd ever seen. *Are you kidding?* Even the soft-boiled eggs I was eating turned hard. Next, she straddled the harp in ways that couldn't possibly be legal. I thought for sure I must be on Candid Camera. The water in the kitchen kettle began boiling, and I hadn't even turned on the stove. This beauty went on for about an hour removing undergarments one by one until only she and the harp in all their natural splendiferous glory remained. I don't think I ever ate a meal so slowly in my entire life. (Hey, I wasn't going anywhere anyway. I was in my robe. Had I stood up and turned, I would have probably knocked all the equipment over.) After the shoot, when I asked the model to join me for dinner that evening, she told me it was really too bad I'd been there for the shoot. She thought I was cute, but now that I had seen her in all her . . . well, beautifulness, she felt funny going out with me. *Who me?* I'd hardly even looked her way! I guess had I been a real rock star instead of just playing one on TV, I would have gotten the girl.

I struck out with her, but I wasn't feeling too badly for myself. I was still basking in the glow of my "rock-star conquest" on my trip down to New Zealand. In what I considered one of my crowning achievements of the time, I wound up sharing a twelve-hour layover with a totally cute flight attendant in her complementary hotel room. (To be totally honest, I have no idea how I pulled this stuff off; I'm certain I couldn't today, nor would I want to. *Hmmm.*)

But even those many years ago, I was already considering putting an end to my womanizing rock-'n'-roll career and getting more serious about my craft and my music (and my life). I knew I was just horsing around and not really finding any answers for myself. Yet, the lure was strong, and somehow I soon found myself sitting on the beach in Aruba playing drums with some pop-rock recording groups from the 1960s. Again, it wasn't about the music; it was all about the lifestyle.

I had my own room right on the beach, was getting paid well, and working just about two hours a night. I didn't know then, but this was to be my rock lifestyle swan song. And what a swan song it was. It was everything all over again, sex, drugs, and rock-'n'-roll—still a hard combination for me to refuse at the time. I settled in for a sweet two-month stay and quickly went to work. At one point I was seeing three women who all knew about each other. It was pretty wild. One was a model from Rio, another I'd seen making out with her girlfriend at a trendy nightclub the week before, and the third was supplying drugs to the band. When the three of them showed up at my beach-side room at the same time for a lunch date, my band buddies wanted to erect a statue in my honor.

I had definitely achieved "cool" status, but in fact, the whole scene was wearing thin for me. A day after the infamous trio showed up, I found myself on the beach, doing my morning "coffee walk" to check out the "action," and I just felt empty. I parked myself on a beach chair, and amidst the passing parade of bikinis, I thought only of home—and my family. My mother had recently died, and although she'd been gone to us for many years, it made me think about my life and what I was doing with it—about who I was, where I came from, and where I was going. I was now in my early thirties, and I was still searching—still trying to be the all-American kid. For all intents and purposes, I had in fact arrived, but the arrival was not as sweet as the promise. I had traveled the world doing my thing, from Hawaii to Europe to Asia—from New Zealand to the Caribbean, and I was still not connected to my true purpose. In the midst of this moment of truth, I received a phone call that would ultimately change the course of my life.

I was offered the lead in a show called "Jonah" at the prestigious Shakespeare Festival for Joseph Papp's Public Theater back in New York. It seemed like someone or something had decided I was indeed through. Not only was this a great opportunity that was tailor made for me (in this retelling of the bible story, Jonah was a drummer who fought with God by singing and playing assorted drum solos), but in an amazing coincidence, the building that housed the Public Theater was originally used as a homeless shelter for Holocaust survivors, and my family lived there when they first arrived in the United States. To clinch the deal, Jonah, which was the name of the show, is my dad's name. It seemed as if the universe were saying, *Yonkee come home.*

I did go home, and I finally began to settle down a bit. I hooked up with one serious girlfriend and began to hone my craft. After a year or so, I actually considered a reprise to my former carousing self after breaking off with my girlfriend—but it seemed there were strange powers at work that were bringing me closer to my final romantic and personal destination.

I was finally coming to the end of my rock-'n'-roll life—but willingly. My search for meaning would continue, but closer to home and with a more internal focus. I knew now that the answers did not lie out there, but within—and I was fortunate to have gotten my wild oats out of my system. To everything there is a time, and my wild time had ended. All of our experiences in life stay with us, and if we're wise, they serve us in our continuing journey. I was grateful that events played out the way they did. Wanderlust and curiosity are not bad things, they just need to be channeled well.

I had come full circle—after all these years, I was back at the place my family had been when they first arrived in this country, when everything was new and scary and unknown. I was the "real" American-born son, now oddly retracing his family's footsteps. When I arrived at the Public Theater on Lafayette Street in Manhattan, I stopped to read the Bronze plaque on the façade of the building. It was dedicated to the Hebrew Immigrant Aid Society (HIAS), which previously occupied the building and housed homeless immigrants arriving from Eastern Europe after the Nazi holocaust. This brought up many mixed feelings, and although I didn't know it at the time, it would mark the beginning of the next chapter of my life professionally and personally, and a period of renewed contact with my family. In a strange way, I had returned home in more ways than one.

Jake Ehrenreich

BASHERT
(or Let Fate Decide)

"Even if your soul mate is predestined,
you still have to make the move."

—Rabbi Shlomo Riskin

JUST FOR THE RECORD, I want it known that I firmly believe our challenge in life is to make the most of what we've been given. While we don't always get to choose our circumstances, we define our lives by the way we behave, the choices we make, and the attitudes we adopt. Attitude and perspective are everything. In that way, we are truly the creators of our journey here on earth. Having said that, it does seem that some things are simply *bashert*— a Yiddish word meaning "meant to be." Take my wife, Lisa, and me, for instance, and the story of our romance.

I was a single musician living in Greenwich Village, and one night, a few musician friends and I decided to go to the Bitter End on Bleeker Street to see a well-known guitarist. My "originals" band had performed at that club fairly often, and it was only a few blocks from my apartment. The Bitter End is one of the most famous and oldest rock-'n'-roll clubs in the world. Performers who had played there include everyone from Bob Dylan to Joni Mitchell to James Taylor to

Billy Joel. The "village" had been filled with famous rock music clubs for many years, like the Café Wha? where I was in the house band and where musicians like Jimi Hendrix, Bruce Springsteen, and many others had gotten their starts. The entire area was a magnet for women, and it was great place for a single musician, such as myself, to live.

That night, as I began to watch the show, my radar went crazy. I had spent so much time scoping chicks that I seemed to have developed a second sense about when a really attractive woman was around. Sure enough, as my consciousness scoured the club for the source of this energy, my eyes were guided to a vision sitting right at the front table—a rock-'n'-roll dream from heaven. Blonde hair and an angel's face, dressed in white T-shirt, blue jeans, and cowboy boots. I must have fallen in love right then and there.

I planned my strategy carefully—if all went well, I would get a chance to speak with her. Sure enough, halfway through the show, she got up to go to the ladies' room. This was what I had been waiting for.

For the uninitiated, the line for the bathroom in a New York City rock club can be really long. At the Bitter End, the line for the ladies' room is just opposite the line for the men's room, in a sort of long hall-way just at the back of the club. If I timed this correctly, I could end up just across from the object of my affection for the entire time in line.

Years of experience paid off. A few moments later, we were just a few feet from each other and not going anywhere fast. I can't recall our conversation exactly, but I'm sure I did my usual song and dance. My specialty was coming across as a combination of the nice guy and the cool, confident musician. I would always try to make myself seem harmless by using some humor as well.

As I remember, Lisa was somewhat reticent to give me her phone number, but I was well prepared for that. In response to her reluctance, I proposed that we let "fate" decide—a term that would later prove prescient. I had developed a foolproof mathematical formula that allowed me to remember phone numbers in my head for about ten to fifteen minutes until I could get to a pen and write them down. I suggested she tell me her phone number once, and only once. If I remembered it, then it was meant to be; if not, then we would be like ships passing in the night. Sleezy, but effective. She went for it.

Lisa and I made some more flirty talk in line until we arrived at our respective destinations. I returned to my seat really excited about this hot chick I had just met.

I called her the next day. No matter how convincing I tried to be, she would just not agree to go out on a date with me! She gave me a lame excuse about getting ready to leave for Australia or some such thing, but I knew she was just giving me the brush off.

I had written her phone number on a flyer from the old Cat Club on Fifteenth Street, and I added my comments: "Looks like Rosanna Arquette." I always wrote comments along with women's phone numbers so I could remember who they were or at least what I thought about them. Being compared to Rosanna Arquette was probably the pinnacle. The actress had recently appeared in *Desperately Seeking Susan* with Madonna and just about every young-blooded American male fell in love with her. Lisa was my Rosanna Arquette.

I was disappointed by the rejection, but I figured, *you win some, you lose some.* I filed Lisa's phone number, along with the numbers on numerous other scraps from other nights, in a special box that I kept in my desk just for that purpose. *Sleezeball.*

A full six years passed without much thought to this gal who got away. About that time, my friend Avi Hoffman had moved into my apartment with me temporarily. His girlfriend Laura (who is now his wife) wanted to fix me up with a gal she thought I might like. She told me that she didn't really know her all that well, but they'd often run into each other at television commercial auditions. She had a gut feeling that we'd hit it off, though, which is why she pressed the matter.

I was never one for being fixed up. Plus, I had just broken up with a girlfriend, and I was considering going back to playing the field a bit (my default setting). I reluctantly agreed to meet Laura's friend but suggested she warn her that I probably wouldn't call for a while.

She lit up and said, "Great. Her name is Lisa Randall—here's her number."

Wait. That sounded really familiar. "Do I know her?" I asked.

She shrugged.

I took the number without further discussion. As soon as Laura left, I pulled out my special box of phone numbers to satisfy my curiosity. Sure enough, there she was: *Lisa Randall*, with the same phone number and my description of Rosanna Arquette!

I remembered her clearly. I was so excited by this "second chance" that I called Lisa right away and left a message. I learned later that when she checked her machine that evening, there were two messages: the first from our mutual friend Laura saying she had given me the number but that Lisa shouldn't expect to get a call from me for a while. And then my message, only moments later.

When Lisa called back the next day, it was clear she had no idea that we had met six years earlier, and I didn't bother to tell her. Why spoil it by reminding her that she had already blown me off? That night, we had a great two-hour phone conversation. We talked about everything from spirituality to music, to the meaning of life, to religion, and we laughed. . . . For goodness sake, my previous girlfriend was hot, but she couldn't even speak English! I was totally blown away, and I also remembered how beautiful I thought Lisa was (she later told me she figured I'd be unattractive, because otherwise the scenario was too good).We ended the exciting phone conversation by setting a date for the following week to get together.

A couple of hours before the date, I couldn't do anything but pace the apartment. I felt like a wreck. My roommate looked worried.

"What's the matter with you?" he asked. "I've never seen you like this."

"I know," I replied. "I'm screwed." I explained that for some inexplicable reason, I was totally freaked out about this date. It's as if something inside me knew I was about to meet my *bashert*—the one who was meant for me. The phone call had been unbelievable, but this was even deeper than that. Something really strange was going on in my universe. We all possess different types of intelligence and different types of insight. This was in my body, not in my head. I think I was *thinking without thinking*. Perhaps an intelligence deep inside me recognized Lisa's soul. Maybe it had to do with some past life relationship. I don't know, I just know how I felt . . . and the feeling was powerful and all-consuming.

Lisa and I began our date by meeting for a drink at Provence, a restaurant on my block. (By the way, I lived on *the* greatest block on earth for a young single guy—MacDougal Street between Houston and Prince, right on the border of Soho and Greenwich Village.) Next, we ate dinner at Japonica on University, and then headed to the Bottom Line to see Tower of Power.

The date was a dream come true. We laughed the kind of laugh that made us know we were attracted to each other—physically and otherwise. We talked easily and there was a great energy between us. They say people emit good pheromones when they're in tune with each other, and ours were slamming. I felt none of the previous nervousness I had in anticipation of the date. And we had so much in common. Lisa loved sushi and she knew a lot about rock music. On top of that, she loved Tower of Power—a funk horn band from the West Coast. But it was more than what we had in common. It was earth-shaking deep.

The last date I had taken to see this band was pretty young. When she asked what kind of band it was, I told her, "Funk."

"Great!" she replied enthusiastically. Then, after a pretty long pause, she asked, "Is that like punk?"

That pretty much summed up a lot of the women I dated for a while. Pretty and sweet. And usually younger than me.

None of that too young stuff with Lisa, though. She was my age, and she knew all about music, too. She talked about drummers playing "tasty" high hats and having a good-sounding "kick drum." This chick had clearly been around. The date was perfect in every way. We shared our first kiss in a doorway a few doors down from the Bottom Line. It was loving and tender and passionate. Not wanting to leave her side for a second, I tried my hardest to convince her to come back with me to my house in the country. Not yet. She said it was too soon to be together like that.

Then, I made the ultimate concession to my newfound love: I drove her back to her apartment in my car! If you've never been to Manhattan, you may require a brief explanation to understand just how big a move it was for me to remove my car from its parking space and drive her home. First of all, very few people who live in Manhattan keep cars—you could pay more for a monthly parking spot than for your apartment. But I needed a car for gigs, so I parked on the street. Parking on the street in Manhattan is *a big drag!* There are *no parking spots*! There were posted signs around NYC that read: DON'T EVEN THINK OF PARKING HERE! I kid you not. Everywhere is illegal—and even if it's not, you'd have to be a NASA scientist to figure that out from the hieroglyphics that pass themselves off as parking regulations.

I joined what I called "the parking club." I became one of those poor wretched souls who get up and out before 7:00 AM each morning to move their cars. Since I had usually come home at 3:00 AM the night before, I was a particularly unhappy member of this fraternity.

Spots were hard to come by, so you had to be tough. Sometimes I wouldn't even have coffee just to get that extra edge. One morning, I had a little episode with one of the local "parking club" guys. I lived in what was still a pretty old-time Italian neighborhood, not far from Little Italy. It was no big secret that there were plenty of "connected" guys around. I was starting to back into a spot, when he tried to get in from behind me. We both got out of the car, and it got heated pretty quickly.

Finally, he looked at me in a telling way. "Look, my friend," he said, slowly and deliberately (it was always bad when they referred to you as "my friend"). "Do yourself a favor. Get back in your car and pull out *now.* I'm parking here."

As luck would have it, we were right in front of the social club where all of his friends hung out, and they'd been watching the whole thing. I had a decision to make. I stood up tall, and as respectfully as I could, I said, "I was here first."

Looking back on it now, I must have been delirious from lack of sleep.

The guy couldn't believe his eyes or ears. Neither could I. *Did I just say that?* My body went numb, and it began to feel as if everything was moving in slow motion. The guy was cool, though. He simply said, "No problem" in that Joe Pesci type of way. Then he did that tough guy walk as he headed for his trunk, no doubt to get his baseball bat. And somehow I don't think he was looking for a pickup game of baseball at 7:00 AM. I feared I had made a bad mistake; I might have to swallow my pride, beg for forgiveness, and move my car quick.

Then from behind me, I heard an angelic voice ring out, "Hey, Frankie, don't be such a fuckin' jerkoff, the kid was there foist, let him have the spot, ya prick." This was true music to my ears. Frankie said a couple of choice words to his friends, and they all began to laugh. He let me have the spot and left me alone.

Believe me when I tell you that moving my car out of a good parking spot to drive Lisa home was a true sign of how quickly and deeply smitten I had become. Once in front of Lisa's apartment, I decided I would let the cat out of the bag and tell her my true identity.

"I know you," I said.

"What do you mean?" she asked doubtfully.

"I know you," I repeated. "We know each other."

"Did I sleep with you and not remember?" was her worrisome response. (Hey, we had lived through the sexual revolution of the sixties and the seventies.)

I explained that we'd met six years earlier at the Bitter End.

"That's not you," she said, clearly confused and concerned.

"Yeah, that's me," I replied.

"No, no. The sleazebag who tried to pick me up that night lives in my neighborhood. I see him occasionally, and I *always* cross the street to avoid him. I've been avoiding him for years!" she explained.

It took some doing, but I finally convinced her that it was me. When I pressed her for the reason she wouldn't accept a date with me back then, she told me it was because I was "really skeevy" and "way too slick." In an odd way, that made me feel pretty good. So, I was *too* cool to date—groovy; turns out she was afraid to tangle with the big boy. To me, being "way too slick" meant "confident and experienced." I still had a lot of self-worth wrapped up in my womanizing prowess.

But it seemed amazing and eerie—almost otherworldly to me that I had "stayed" in Lisa's consciousness through her avoidance of this other guy she'd mistaken for me, for six long years. I would have imagined she never thought of me again. And now it seemed as if fate had indeed brought us together for a second chance.

Why had Lisa given me her correct phone number when we first met if she thought I was skeevy and slick? And why would a friend she barely knew offer to set her up with me? Why had I "stayed" in her life for so long? Some might say it was *bashert* and that there were some other powers at work. I don't know, but sometimes old wives' tales and ancient beliefs can hold much wisdom.

Lisa and I fell deeply in love, and the rest, as they say, is history. Just for the record . . . a few weeks after our dream date, it was Lisa's birthday. I dropped hints after only the first week about possibly asking her to marry me on her birthday, mere weeks after we met. We both knew this was it. But in the end, it was just too quick, and I couldn't trust it. The day came and went, and it seemed I wasn't yet ready to go off into that good night.

It actually took three long tumultuous years before Lisa and I finally had our nuptials, but, as they say, good things are worth waiting for.

UNCONDITIONAL LOVE
(or The Most Tender Part of the Heart)

*"Until one has loved an animal, a part of
one's soul remains unawakened."*

—Anatole France

MUCH OF WHAT I KNOW about love—especially unconditional love—I learned over the years from my many animal companions. In the years before we got married, Lisa often complained that I would give the most tender part of my love to my dog. That was probably true, but it made sense to me. I've always felt that dogs and other animals were innocent and without guile, in contrast to humans, who seem to require further analysis.

I rescued my dog Monster off a highway at three in the morning on my way home to Manhattan from a gig singing at a Russian night-club in Brooklyn. I noticed him walking along the side of Ocean Parkway, and it just didn't look right. If you're in tune with animals, especially dogs, you can see in their faces and by their gait whether or not they are lost. He looked lost, and I knew he'd probably end up getting hit by a car, so I pulled off the road and approached him. He was a little skittish at first, but I was able to make him trust me. I tied a rope I had in the car to his collar (no tags!) and walked him around the neighborhood trying to get some signal from him about where he belonged. It was hard to tell what kind of dog he was at the time, because oddly, all his hair was totally shaven off. He was a pretty big dog, with a sweet golden retriever/German shepherd–type face, but with all his hair gone, he just looked crazy. In fact, that's how I came to call him Monster. I wasn't making any progress finding his home, so I reluctantly decided to take him home with me and start calling the dog pounds the next day.

After a few weeks of unsuccessful attempts to find his owner, I decided to keep him and spent many wonderful years training him. He was never on a leash, and I could stop him in midrun just by calling his name—even if he were chasing a squirrel or some other animal. I worked with him at the dog run in Washington Square Park, with a dozen or so dogs running haywire while we trained, and that made all the difference. His focus on me was so beautiful, and people would often comment on our relationship. We were true friends who loved each other in that uniquely special cross-species way that animal lovers know.

Years later, when Monster lost his battle with cancer, I was devastated. After trying every possible cure, I finally had the vet come to my home to help him out of his misery. Several friends who loved Monster came to the house as well, and we finished off a couple of bottles of 1956 Hooper's vintage port in his honor. We told stories of him before we buried him in the yard along with other pets who had passed away.

Lisa and I were living together at the time, and she was nearing her wits end with my seeming unwillingness to tie the knot. Monster's death put me in a particularly emotional place, and it made me think long and hard about a lot of things, especially what Lisa had said about my most tender love going to him.

While it was true that animals are innocent and deserve unconditional love, it was also a conveniently safe place for me to put that love. I knew for sure that my dogs or cats would never reject me; their love was truly unconditional. I came to see that it was now time to move to the next stage of my life and undertake the challenge of offering that type of love to a human being. My choice was to either get another dog or take the plunge. I loved Lisa deeply, and I finally decided I would ask her to marry me on Valentine's Day, which was the next day.

I immediately went to tell my father of my decision. He had been waiting for years for me to ask Lisa to marry me. My sisters had never married and now that seemed pretty much out of the picture because of their psychological problems. I was my dad's only hope for continuing the family line.

"Dad, I'm going to ask Lisa to marry me tomorrow," I told him proudly, sure he would be as excited as I felt.

"Tomorrow, tomorrow . . . it's always tomorrow with you," he complained.

"No, Dad, I'm serious," I explained. "I mean literally *tomorrow*."

"Again with tomorrow, always tomorrow. What's wrong with today?" he asked.

"Tomorrow's Valentine's Day. I thought that would be cool," I said, sure now he would understand.

"There's always some excuse with you," he replied. He still wasn't getting it.

"Okay," I agreed. "Okay, I guess today is okay. I'll ask Lisa to marry me today."

It took a moment, but when he realized I was serious, he could barely contain his joy. He had waited much of his adult life for one of his children to get married, and after years of disappointment, it was finally happening. I asked him to take out the box of my mother's old jewelry we'd been saving since she'd gotten sick. The two of us combed through it with the anticipation of a child who'd discovered a secret treasure chest, and I'll never forget the shared feeling of excitement that this day had actually come. I wanted to present Lisa with something special, and as she'd never met my mom, a ring with my mother's energy in it would be perfect. We found an antique platinum ring, with two rows of round and baguette diamonds across the front that we all thought would work (by this time my father's wife, Ruth, had joined in the festivities), but the ring was old and tarnished, and badly needed to be cleaned. It couldn't be presented as it was. I went to a jeweler in town and asked him to clean it up and prepare it for action. When he told me it would take a few days to clean it properly, I was devastated. We ended up choosing a beautiful ring, just for show, to use for the proposal (thank God I didn't really have to buy that thing). I would tell Lisa about the real ring from my mom and transfer the rings a few days later.

I went home and waited in excited anticipation for Lisa to come back from work. In an odd coincidence, she had taken a part-time job as a makeup artist at the Nevele Hotel in the Catskills, just about forty minutes from where we lived. When Lisa didn't arrive home at her usual time, I became concerned, but not overly so—not yet, anyway. I figured she probably stopped at the supermarket, so I decided I would go find her and surprise her. I went to all the places in town where she shopped—no Lisa. And it was way after her usual arrival time. Now I became seriously worried. Visions of my long-ago first night in a Catskills hotel came whizzing through my brain. It was so easy to get a room at one of those places! What if Lisa had finally had enough of my procrastinating and was at this very moment giving in to some persistent suitor, who she had put off for so long, just waiting for me to come around. My head was in a whirl. After all the years of searching, to have finally found *the one* and have her slip away at the very last moment . . . what was I thinking? Why had I waited so long? I had said many times to Lisa that although I knew it was right, it wasn't perfect, and we still had problems. Lisa would say that people don't get to pick whether or not they have problems in a relationship; they all do. We only get to pick which set of problems we choose to deal with. That's why I loved her so. She was not only beautiful, but very wise. And now she was gone! (She was funny, too. When asked on our wedding day what it felt like to finally be getting married for the first time at age thirty-nine, Lisa said, "You know, at this age, it's not that long a commitment anymore.") And now I had blown it! What a putz! I had found love, and let it go. I was a mess.

When Lisa finally pulled up at our home, I was so relieved. I wanted to ask her to marry me right then just to make sure I never "lost" her again. (I really felt like saying, "Thank God you're alive!" *Wham.*) But I waited for dinner.

We went to our favorite Japanese restaurant (this was a theme for us). I waited until after the *uni* arrived (raw sea urchin gonads). I figured if it was good that night that would be a good omen. It was perfect. I began to talk lovingly about our dog Monster, who had just passed away, and how I loved him—and I talked about life in general and how important our journey was—eventually I got to how grateful I was to have found her, and I told her how much I loved her, and always had—from the moment I first saw her. She must have known something was up (how could she not?)—but she didn't let on if she did. Finally, right there, on the eve of Valentine's Day, I proposed marriage to my beloved, my *bashert.*

"Lisa, will you marry me?" I asked.

Her reaction was straight out of Romeo and Juliet: "What do you mean?" she responded.

Perhaps this was not going to be as easy as I thought after all. I was taken aback. Of all the responses I anticipated Lisa might give, this was not one. Based on our relationship and our umpteen discussions about marriage, I had always just assumed she would say "yes," or some version of yes, as in *"Oh yes, yes, yes . . . I've waited all my life for my true love to come, and now yes, yes, oh, one thousand times yes!"* Somehow "What do you mean?" threw me. Might she actually be saying no? I came back with the only response I could muster at the time.

"What do you mean, *what do you mean?*" was my brilliant retort. But then, to save the moment I continued, "I'm asking you to marry me . . . to be my wife." I remembered how I felt just a few hours earlier when I thought she was out of my life, and I was not about to let her go again.

Lisa seemed a little flustered herself.

"Well . . . get down on one knee," she insisted.

For goodness sake, we were at the sushi bar (I know, I know . . . but we came at the last minute with no reservations, and there were no tables). I did get down on one knee, and Lisa finally said yes. I can't remember much after that. I was too happy and relieved, but I'm pretty sure there was a round of applause at the bar.

Lisa and I always celebrate Valentine's Day on the eve of the holiday in honor of our engagement, which works out when making dinner reservations. Plus, it is a celebration of our love all on our own, and I have my dad to thank for that for "pushing" me into it.

A week or so after our engagement, we were having a dinner party for my fortieth birthday at our house. This was a big day—Lisa was preparing a six-course wine-tasting meal featuring lamb roast as the main course, and my sommelier friend had chosen separate wines for each course.

We thought it would be the perfect opportunity to announce the exciting news to our closest friends. There were fourteen of us that night, and most had been waiting several years for me to finally get up the guts to ask Lisa to marry me. Our friends all knew my checkered history with women, but they also knew that Lisa was the "one." They mocked my "but, it's not perfect" excuse for delaying the inevitable by posting a sheet on the fridge entitled "How's Lisa doing today?" that I was supposed to fill out each day.

After the toasts and just before dinner, I began speaking tenderly about my beautiful dog and our relationship, and about unconditional love. I spoke about relationships in general, about personal growth and vulnerability, and about the challenges and importance of giving and sharing love. Basically, I was going over some of the same territory I traveled when I proposed. No one had any idea where I was going with this. I told the story of my epiphany after Monster's death and how it led to my proposing to Lisa. When I finally let out the news, the place went nuts. It was pandemonium—lots of hugs and kisses and laughter and tears. Then, at just the right moment, a close friend, who we all knew had been having marital problems, turned to her husband and loudly proclaimed, "Maybe we should get a dog and kill it." There was a brief silence, and then the table exploded with laughter.

Fast forward six months. Our wedding day was right out of a storybook. We rented a small inn in the Catskill Mountains and brought our closest family and friends for the weekend. We had the wedding and the reception on Saturday evening. It was the middle of July, a great time of year for an outdoor wedding—but we were about to be visited by hurricane Bertha.

The morning of our wedding, Lisa woke me at about 6:00 AM, saying, "Sweetheart, I have something to tell you."

Now, I don't know about you, but about the last thing I had ever wanted to hear from my fiancé on our wedding day is, *"Sweetheart, I have something to tell you."* All kinds of stuff went racing through my mind. *She's a guy. She slept with my father*—and that's the mild stuff—you don't want to know. Hey, I was sleeping! It turns out Lisa woke me to say that the tent for the reception had blown down during the night. I think she was a little confused by my relief at the news.

It was touch and go all day. We had planned a beautiful outdoor dusk to evening ceremony, lit only by dozens of torches. Unfortunately, the wind and rain continued, and we decided to move everything indoors. But, at the last moment, there was a break in the weather. Although the sky was more ominous than I'd ever seen it, I took it as a sign to proceed. I told the staff to bring everything back outside. They thought I was nuts (which I probably was . . . it was *cold* and really crazy weather), but I didn't care. I had a feeling, and I was right—

the rain held off just long enough for us to complete our ceremony.

My father and Ruth, Joanie and Wanda, Lisa's sister, her brother-in-law, aunt and uncle, and other wedding guests waited outside in anticipation of our arrival. At the start of the ceremony we invoked the name of all my relatives who had passed and invited them to join us. My mother, my grandparents, all the aunts and uncles and children murdered in the Shoah—and Lisa's family, too: her mother and grandfather and others. The sky was lit by the setting sun, which filtered through the eerie and haunting clouds as we stood underneath our *chuppah*, our wedding canopy—made from my prayer shawl and held above us on wooden poles by our closest friends. The innkeeper watched from the roof of the old Victorian mansion, and swore he could feel the presence of many souls in the air—a presence he had never felt before or since.

Lisa circled around me seven times in the traditional and mysterious ancient rite meant to create a safe space for our lives. She in her white dress, and me in my white robe or *kittel*—both of us pure and born anew in our bond. We spoke our vows to confirm the *ketubah* or marriage contract we had signed just a short while earlier and broke the glass in the ancient traditional ceremony some believe is to ward off evil spirits. But there were no evil spirits that night—my spirit family made sure of that.

During the evening reception, my dad got up to make a speech. I had never seen him as happy as he was on this night. One of his children was finally getting married—his simple dream come true at last. But he was so moved he simply could not speak or see the words it had taken him all weekend long to write. I joined him and read them for him as he held a candle for me to read by. My father wrote a beautiful letter in which he talked of our family and our history, and of Lisa, and of his hopes and dreams for our lives—and in which he said that "although this was such a joyous occasion, and we had a tent full of people—there should be ten tents full of people," and he said that Lisa and I "were the rightful inheritors of the unfinished lives of those who perished."

Somehow I feel as though my family "heard" that speech that night. That in some strange way, they had "arranged" to be there under cover of the hurricane—and maybe even had been active, say, in a young man and woman's life some years earlier—and "arranged" other things as well. And perhaps their spirit would simply not be denied, that there would be someone to carry on this family, that there would be another "rightful inheritor" in the world—our son. The first step had been taken—but where it would take us is another story.

FAMILY

(or Why Don't I Have a Grandmother?)

*"The bond that links your true family
is not one of blood, but of respect
and joy in each other's life."*

—Richard Bach

"**F**AMILY" CAN MEAN MANY DIFFERENT THINGS
to many different people. There is the traditional family, and
ever more common, the nontraditional family. There is family related
by blood, family created by marriage, and people who just "feel" like
family. Ultimately, family are those people from whom you get
love—the people who "have your back." I had a nontraditional family
way before it was fashionable.

About fifty years ago, I asked my dad why I didn't have a grandmother. I have long since forgotten the incident, but my father
recounted it in his testimony for Steven Spielberg's Shoah Foundation
and in a 1988 newspaper article he had published in the *Times Herald
Record*.* As my dad tells it, I was about four years old at the time. My
friend's grandmother had called him in for some treats, and I ran
home crying. That's when I asked my dad how come I didn't have a
grandmother, too.

**The text of this article is included on pages 247–250.*

Although my dad gave me some response about Hitler and the Holocaust, I never really got a satisfactory answer from him. But, then again, what could you tell a four-year-old boy so that he would understand? I'm not sure I would know how to answer either. Still, although my father ultimately became a great scholar, writer, and teacher of Yiddish, the Holocaust, and other subjects, he *never* spoke of his family (*my* family!) or his life before or during the war when I was growing up. This was in sharp contrast to my mother, who always seemed to want to talk, especially about the family she lost—her brother and sister, her parents and grandparents. But, somehow, my sisters and I knew instinctively during our childhood not to bring the subject up with my dad. The question from that four-year-old boy might have been the last time we discussed it until I became a young adult.

When I was nineteen years old, I traveled the world performing on the *S. S. Rotterdam*. While away from home, I finally summoned the courage to write a letter to my dad, in which I asked him straight out why he never spoke of his family or his childhood home, or of those days at all.

To my surprise, he wrote back a very sad, but very beautiful letter in which he explained that he didn't talk about his past because he feared "his words would pale in comparison to who and what was lost."

I was very moved by those words. I had no idea my father harbored those feelings. They seemed way more sentimental than I ever imagined he was. I began to suspect how much sadness was buried out of sight, and in fact, it all came pouring out years later in his writings and lectures. I'm glad he was able to fulfill what he ultimately came to see as his survivor's obligation to tell the story of what had happened.

Even though my father never talked about his family when we were young, he and my mother had the mindfulness to provide me and my sisters with a "nontraditional" family from the very beginning. My sisters and I grew up with no grandparents, and no "real" aunts, uncles, or first cousins—but we had people who became family-member surrogates. Many survivor families like mine were able to build relationships with other survivor families, which created genuine family bonds. While we were never able to conjure up grandparents, we somehow ended up with aunts, uncles, and cousins. These "relatives" were actually people my family connected with in Russia during the war and afterward at displaced persons camps in Germany. Although we knew we weren't related by blood, these were real family to us, and we got love and a sense of connection from them.

Two main families became "ours": the Waxmans and the Ofmans. My mom used to tell us a story about when the three families were in line to catch a train somewhere in Russia. Wanda got ill, and my mother was late getting to the train. This was an extremely tenuous time and somehow catching this train was some big deal. I can't remember the story exactly, but this part stuck with me: The Waxmans and Ofmans pulled themselves and their valises off the train and would not leave until my mother arrived—they would go together or not at all. Those are the kinds of people who became family. (I once went to my dad's house and found that same type of valise—which he later used to come to the United States—by the garbage pickup out in front of the house. It was marked *Jojne Ehrenreich USA*. I grabbed it and brought it into his home and asked him just what he thought he was doing with it. It turns out in response to pressure about being such a packrat, he was attempting to clean house a bit and decided to throw it away. "It's an old valise," he said, "and I don't think anybody's really going to use it anymore." *No kidding.* I shook my head in disbelief that he would get rid of this irreplaceable family heirloom because my wife and I might not use it to go to Florida. I gently told him to consult me before throwing away anything else.)

When we were kids, my sisters and I always knew when one of these two families was phoning us because my mother—who usually answered the phone—would launch into a wild cavalcade of Yiddish hysterics. *"Oy. . . . How are you? . . . The children? . . . The family? . . . Oy! . . . It's so wonderful to hear your voice. . . . Oy!"*

I recall one evening in particular when she answered the phone. She went through her litany of questions and responses, squealing, yodeling, yakking, clucking, and gesticulating wildly. This went on for about fifteen minutes. Finally, she handed the phone over to my dad. He got on the line and made some very warm general pleasantries for a few minutes, then said good-bye and hung up.

He turned to my mother and said, "Who was that?"

"I don't know—why didn't you ask?" she replied.

Dumbfounded, my father shot back, "You were on the phone for fifteen minutes! How could I ask, *Who are you? You* should have asked!"

They argued back and forth like this for the entire evening. It was like growing up with bad Yiddish theater in my kitchen.

But in a way, I came to see that it really didn't matter if it had been the Ofmans or the Waxmans on the phone, because what these families shared in common almost transcended who they were as individuals. My parents would have had the same sincere sentiments for both families.

Over the years, the Waxman and the Ofman families prospered and continued to grow. There were grandchildren and in-laws and a growing extended family network. By contrast, our family had none of that. My sisters never married, and I was traveling around the world, with little prospects of settling down. And all too soon, we had our illnesses to contend with—which consumed our lives. Staying in close contact became more difficult, and as time went by, the families became further out of touch—but never entirely so. Both couples traveled to New York to see my mom when she was ill, and you can still see the pain in their faces when viewing the photos from those visits.

When Lisa and I got engaged and were planning our wedding, we reestablished contact with the families and were fortunate to have many "family" members attend. We were as welcoming to each other as if we were real family—because we were.

Later, at a Waxman wedding, Duvid (my "uncle") took Lisa aside, and he was so warm and gregarious and loving with her—even though he had never met her before; she was Yankele's wife, that's all that mattered. He expressed to Lisa how much affection he had for our family and how sorry he felt for my father for having had no grandchildren—but he knew she would fix that! Without prompting, he proceeded to tell her she was pregnant . . . and with a boy. We had no idea at the time that Lisa was pregnant, but a week later we returned home to find he was exactly right. That's the kind of thing that only a relative does—some warm, loving, eccentric aunt or uncle. It was so incredibly special to have Duvid talk with my wife that way, and it brought back some of the eery, otherwordly feelings I felt at our wedding.

The bond remains deep with both families, and we continue to honor our parents' memory by keeping our relationships alive.

There's a lot of debate these days about what type of families are acceptable and what type are not. Ultimately, people—especially children—need love and connection as the primary force in their life. And love is love. Any honest human beings who are willing to give of themselves to share love are true family. Whoever "has your back," as they say. Sometimes they can even fill the void of "real" family. I know they did for me.

THE BIRTH

(or Giving New Life to the Family Name)

"What does labor feel like?
Take your lower lip and pull it over your head."
                                                    —Carol Burnett

THE BIRTH OF A CHILD into any family is a monumental occasion—a celebration of life and a brief glimpse into the mysteries and wonders of existence. Notwithstanding my obvious bias on the subject, the birth of my son, Dovy, was something very special and incredibly significant.

Dovy is the first and only grandchild of our survivor family. My father was eighty years old in 1998 when he was born—his only proof that Hitler did not succeed in exterminating his and my mother's entire bloodline. My son's given name is Joseph Dov-Behr, for two of his great uncles who perished in the Holocaust. (Together, my parents had eight brothers and sisters between them, none of whom survived the war.) As I've explained, my sisters, Joanie and Wanda, never married nor had children. To add to that, Lisa's mom died at age thirty-five, when Lisa was just eleven, after which her father sort of freaked out. (I guess he did his best, but by the time Lisa was fifteen, she was on her own). Lisa's younger brother's whereabouts are unknown, her older sister married but had no children, and her grandfather committed suicide. So, in other words, Dovy (his nickname) is the only grandchild on both sides of broken families—a precious kid.

As soon as we were married, Lisa and I started trying to have a child right away. Lisa was thirty-nine, and I was forty (first marriages for both of us . . . a miracle!). We had three pregnancies in the space of a year, including two miscarriages. During our third pregnancy, we were so nervous, we decided to go to a fertility specialist. Lisa always enjoyed giving the information to the nurse in the waiting room, who would ask each patient before escorting her to the correct room, "In vitro?" Lisa would proudly answer, "Intercourse."

The doctor couldn't find anything wrong but cited recent studies suggesting slow thyroid function as a possible factor in miscarriage (Lisa was borderline). We tried a small dose of Synthroid, and Lisa held this baby to term. However, the trial of errors that saw our Dovy actually enter this world is another story.

Lisa and I are both pretty alternative when it comes to health and health care. It's not that we don't recognize the value of traditional Western care; we just feel we'd like to make the best use of all avenues available to us. For instance, if I break my arm, I don't want someone giving me herbs except to help my body heal *after* the arm is set in a cast. And thank goodness for antibiotics, *but only when you really need them*, not as a cure-all. We are all aware, or should be, that the overuse of antibiotics and other useful medicines and techniques wreak havoc on our health and our healthcare system.

So, Lisa and I decided to go as natural as possible with our child's birth. After moving around a little, we settled with a practice that featured two midwives and a doctor. Mostly we would be attended to by the midwives, but we would have the doctor as backup if we needed him. We studied the Bradley method of natural childbirth very seriously. Bradley views birth as a natural process (no drugs) and supports education, preparation, and a loving, supportive coach. I learned more than I ever wanted to know about the human reproductive system.

Although we did sonograms and even an amniocentesis, we didn't want to know our child's sex before the birth. Each checkup would begin with me frantically spouting out, before our practitioner could speak a word, "Remember, we don't want to know the gender," lest they forget and blurt out "she" or "he" by mistake.

We wanted to give birth as naturally as possible, and preferably somewhere other than a hospital, but we also wanted to feel safe, especially given our history and Lisa's "high-risk" status due to her age (she was forty-one). We found several "birthing cottages" and finally settled on one that was located on the grounds of a hospital— just what the doctor ordered. In the cottage, birthing was all natural, with no drugs. If necessary, transfer to the hospital was child's play, so to speak, as it was only a few hundred yards away.

There is a very wise Yiddish saying that best describes our birthing experience: *"Der mentsh trakht un got lakht,"* which roughly translates to "People plan and God laughs." Sort of like the English saying, "Best laid plans of mice and men." After all our planning and studying, things didn't go quite the way we had intended.

Contractions started the night of the big 1998 NY Knicks/Miami Heat NBA playoff game. I love basketball; I played high school and some college, yet I was never really a big professional sports fan as an adult. But the Knicks still held a special place for me, with memories of Walt "Clyde" Frazier, Earl "The Pearl" Monroe, and our warrior captain Willis Reed hobbling onto the court in game seven of the NBA championships to inspire a win over the mighty Lakers. And no one who lived in New York City could forget 1969, when the Mets, Jets, and Knicks went all the way! Yes, even if only for old time's sake, a Knick playoff game was still something to be excited about.

We were told to keep a log of the time between contractions before heading off for the hospital, so we wouldn't arrive too early. I collated my birthing notes with the running score of the game. My notes read: *8:10 Lisa had a 30-second contraction; KNICKS SCORE! Up by 2!*

After many hours of home labor, we arrived at the birthing cottage with our scented candles and our Bradley training. One midwife was there to meet us. We settled in, and we labored . . . and labored . . . and the midwives had a change in shift . . . and we labored . . . and labored some more. . . .

After thirty-six hours of questionable "progression," two midwife shift changes, and methods like warm showers (I got in, too!), lots of walking around, and a few enemas (not me) to move the process along, we all finally decided perhaps it would be wise to move to the hospital just to get a little Pitocin, which causes uterine contractions, to help get things going. This led to more Pitocin, and then ultimately, to the tender and sensitive motherly sentiments that can often accompany this type of birth: *"Get this thing out of me!"*

Well, *things* were simply not moving; the kid didn't seem like he was in any rush to say, "What's up, Doc?" At the midwife's suggestion, the decision was made to call the doctor. Of course, Lisa ended up having a Cesarean section. At some point, it just became about

Lisa and the baby's safety and everyone surviving what had truly become an ordeal.

We didn't know the sex of our baby until the doctor handed him to me in the operating room. I couldn't believe we had a healthy baby boy. I imagined Lisa was pleased, but to be honest, it was a little hard to tell between her bouts of throwing up.

I followed the kid around like a hawk.

"No silver nitrate in his eyes please."

"No, he won't be getting the hepatitis-C vaccination at birth."

"Yes, I promise we'll be seeing a pediatrician."

Some of the procedures in a hospital nursery are designed for the general public welfare. This is the only time a doctor will see some of these kids, but that did not apply to us.

Lisa and Dovy would have to stay in the hospital for about four days while Lisa recouped from her unexpected surgery. But there was a problem: Although the hospital was enlightened enough to partner with a birthing cottage on the grounds, they had not yet updated their maternity unit in the hospital itself. I had somehow talked my way into the operating room during the birth of my son, but now there were no provisions for me to stay with my wife and son overnight, or for that matter, even after normal visiting hours. Oops.

I believe very strongly in personal responsibility, and I think many of us give it up too easily to others. Although I was sure no one at this hospital sought to harm my wife or child in any way, I was not about to leave them with strangers at this time in our lives. In fact, one nurse had asked me why I was keeping such a close eye on my son earlier that day.

"What do you think we're going to do to him?" she asked.

I replied that I was sure they would do nothing but what they thought was right and correct, but that this was *my* son and his welfare was ultimately my responsibility. This is how I felt about Lisa as well. They were both in no position to care for themselves, and since we know that mistakes happen at hospitals as in other parts of life, I would simply stay to be their advocate. If anything happened to either one of them while I wasn't there, I would never forgive myself.

No, I decided that whatever it took, I would be staying.

Visiting hours were coming to an end; the nurses were making their rounds, and I was advised that I would have to get ready to leave. I tried to explain as gently and quietly as possible that I really felt I needed to stay. I had arranged for Dovy to be in the room with us, and I could very easily keep an eye on them both. I would be helpful. There were no other patients in the room. I promised I would be no trouble.

No such luck.

The nurse got her supervisor who proceeded to reinforce in no uncertain terms that I must leave the hospital. In a strange non sequitur, she eerily reminded me of Miss Sazooly, the lunchroom monitor at my junior high school, but without the massive ring of keys hanging from her belt. I found the midwife. She knew our birth plan was so much different; after all, the birthing cottage would have had us all together until we went home, even with Lisa not having had major surgery. I simply felt I had to stay. She explained she had very little power in the hospital, but she found the doctor for me. I asked him to please intervene.

He returned telling me that he had done his best, but it was against hospital policy. He couldn't promise anything.

The head nurse returned. I would have to leave. Decision time.

I calmly explained to the nurse in charge (the Miss Sazooly look-alike) that I understood she was simply doing her job. I detailed that I was a sane and rational person who was only doing what he felt he must to help insure the safety of his young family. I didn't want any trouble. I explained the special significance of my son and our Holocaust family. I practically begged and assured them over and over that I would be absolutely no trouble. I would sleep on the floor next to Lisa's bed, out of sight. They could pretend I was not there during nonvisiting hours.

I was getting nowhere, so I also explained the alternative.

If they continued to insist that I leave, they would have to call the state police to have me removed, and while they did, I would make the entire ward miserable by basically going nuts. I had threatened this once before when my dad was in the hospital and the nurse wouldn't let me call the doctor in an emergency at 3:00 AM. It had worked then, and I hoped it would work here.

A conference took place in the hallway between administrators and health professionals, and then they all just disappeared. It seemed they had tacitly agreed to a sort of nonaggression pact, and I was being permitted to stay, at least for now.

Good to my word, I refrained from sleeping in the unused bed in the room and slept on the floor between the bed and the wall, out of sight. Good to their word, the staff totally ignored the fact that I was there during nonvisiting hours and spoke to me only during pre-scribed visiting times. It was actually pretty comical and surreal to be walking around as if I were invisible. I felt like Patrick Swayze in the movie *Ghost*. I ate very little and washed less. I was there for four days and nights.

On the second day, my dad and Ruth came to visit. I had them bring me a change of clothes, and I met them about ten miles from the hospital so they could follow me to the place. (This was ages before GPS.)

My father had waited for as long as I can remember for this moment, and I had never seen him happier. He looked at Dovy, then at me. He couldn't stop saying how beautiful he was. "This is a beautiful kid . . . this is some kid . . . what a beautiful kid," he crowed. Then he turned to me. "You were an ugly kid."

My father and I were unusually close by that time of my life. He looked deep in my eyes and said, "You know how much I love you, but I cannot describe to you the love of a grandparent for a grandchild."

He'd certainly waited long enough. Before Dovy was born, I remembered how my father would come home from some celebration, a wedding or bar mitzvah, and friends had shown him pictures of their grandchildren. He told me it cut through him like a knife, and in fact, he finally stopped attending celebrations altogether because it was simply too painful.

The relationship my father and son shared, albeit for a brief time, was truly otherworldly—and not just in my opinion. A dear friend of mine was visiting with her mother, who is a grandmother as well. I later learned that on the way home from my house, my friend's mother turned to her and said, "I love your children, but I have never ever seen anything like the way that man looks at that child."

The rabbi at my dad's funeral, when speaking to my son during the eulogy said, "It is very possible, Dovy, that no one in the history of the world has been as loved and as adored by anyone as you were by your zeyde." All the tenderness and love that my father was unable to show me or my sisters in our early lives poured into Dovy. Our family would continue after all.

A few days after the birth, I bid farewell to my sleeping spot on the floor—it was finally time to go home. I began by carrying down all of the flowers that had been sent to the hospital. I put the flowers next to me in the backseat and began figuring out how to put in my first baby car seat. I've always enjoyed deciphering directions that seem to have been written by a third party who was translating for somebody's sister who once knew a taxi driver that actually spoke English.

It was mid-May, a warm and sunny day. I had the windows and the sunroof open wide. As I was attempting to put the seat in the car, I was being badgered by what seemed like unusually aggressive wasps and bees. I got stung twice.

I brilliantly deduced that I must be parked near a nest or hive of some kind, so I moved the car to another area of the parking lot. I resumed the task of securing the car seat in the back with the windows wide open. Gee, the wasps must have followed me. I got stung three more times. Now my face and lip were swollen and bloody.

I was a new father. I was in a state of bliss. I guess I could be excused for not realizing that the wasps were simply attracted to all the scented flowers I had stashed right next to my head as I tried to install the car seat in the back. I can only imagine the peals of laughter emanating from any sadistic bystander who may have witnessed this comic tragedy. Even I began laughing at my own stupidity when I finally realized what was happening. To be honest, I don't think anything could have truly bothered me that day.

In a flash of insight, I shooed the wasps out, closed the windows, turned on the AC, and miraculously figured out how to install the seat.

When I finally returned to the room, I had been gone quite a long time. Lisa saw my swollen, bloody face and gasped, "Oh my God, were you in a fight?"

As we laughed in the car on the way home, I was so blissful, even the stings didn't bother me. And I'm proud to say I didn't kill a single wasp that day.

My life has never been the same.

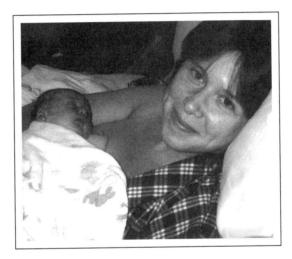

THE BRIS

(or It's No Laughing Matter)

"It's déjà vu all over again."

—Yogi Berra

I **AM NOT A TRADITIONALIST** where religion is concerned, mine or anybody else's. I have my own ideas about spirituality, and everyone else is entitled to their own. Although it can be, organized religion is not *necessarily* spiritual. These are large groups, and as such, they often have their own agendas. I seek out truth where I may find it, and there is usually a piece of it in many places—in and out of the great organized religions. I seek to *live* in the spirit of eternal wisdom teachings, as opposed to blindly following dogma.

There is, however, a very important aspect to organized religion and its customs that cannot be easily dismissed. The physical traditions and proscribed holidays and observances serve as an effective vehicle for transmission of ethics and values and culture from one generation to the next. They can also make us feel rooted and connected to a people and a tradition and foster a feeling of belonging. In addition, if done properly, it can help to keep the family unit cohesive and create lasting traditions within families that may go a long way toward strengthening those ties. Many of these traditions are beautiful and easy to adhere to—some are more challenging.

The days following Dovy's birth were full of joy and wonder, if not sleep. Lisa was still recovering from her surgery, and I was basically taking care of them both. I can't count the number of times I checked to see if Dovy was still breathing. I'm a bit embarrassed to say I did this for years and sometimes still do even now while he's sleeping. Force of habit, I guess.

Eight days after the birth of a Jewish boy, it is customary to have a traditional circumcision, or *bris* as it is called in Yiddish. This is the traditional age-old fulfillment of God's covenant with the children of Abraham.

One of my favorite Yiddish expressions involves this tradition. If you ask someone, *"Vos makhstu?"* it literally means, "What do you make?" but is meant to mean, "How are you doing?" Playful responses to this question number pretty high. One of my favorites is *"Ikh makh a bris!"* ("I'm making a bris!") This response always seems joyful, colloquial, playful, hopeful, and *heymish* (homey).

Much to Lisa's dismay, I decided that Dovy's bris should be a joyful community celebration at our home. We would fill our home with photos of our lost relatives and invite the entire community and everyone we knew. Many times families will just invite their circle of friends, but given the importance of our son, and the love of the community for my father, we just made it an open invitation. Lisa was still not really out of bed from her surgery, and this would certainly be a crazy day at our home, but I was not to be deterred. She still describes our son's bris as one of the worst days of her life. Which, I will say, is understandable.

A bris is really no laughing matter. After all, surgery is being performed on your eight-day-old son right in your living room, while people are milling around eating bagels and lox. If it wasn't so serious, it might actually be funny. I think I might be okay with it if the surgery was on the finger, or the arm, or anywhere for that matter except where it actually is. (I'm still convinced they took the biggest part of what I had.)

The person who performs the bris is called a *mohel* (pronounced *moil.*). This is a rabbi especially trained for this task. We got our guy by calling 1-800-BABYBOY. I kid you not.

As you might imagine, there are innumerable jokes about mohels, which reminds me . . .

I was in the men's room the other day and I turned to the guy in the stall next to me.

"Hey, mister," I began, "were you circumcised by Moishe the cock-eyed mohel?"

"Yes," he said, somewhat taken aback. "How did you know?"

"You're peeing on my leg."

Bada boom.

I went to a bris and the mohel was selling a wallet for a thousand dollars.

I was stunned. "A wallet for a thousand dollars?"

The mohel explained he fashioned this wallet from the tips he'd saved from his circumcisions. "If you rub it, it turns into a suitcase."

I'm available by calling 1-800-BADJOKE. (I kid you, yes.)

To be honest, as the date approached, I started to have second thoughts about the whole bris thing. Why should it be right to cut off a piece of this poor kid's penis at eight days old? No kidding, it just seemed barbaric to me. I know a lot of people in the United States do it now—even if they're not Jewish, for hygiene and so on—but it still wasn't sitting so well with me. After all, this is my son, and I'm responsible for him.

The night before the bris, I called my own rabbi in desperation. "Garry, I'm having some reservations about the bris. Do you know anyone who doesn't do this?"

"No Jew I know" was his response. And this was from a reform rabbi—the most progressive and liberal branch of Judaism. My father also pointed out that, in the thousands of years of Jewish history, even the most assimilated Jews kept the covenant. I continued to give the matter some serious thought. In the end, I decided that given my family's Holocaust history and those Jews who gave their lives just for the sake of being Jewish, I would not be the one to break the most fundamental of all the Jewish traditions. Yet, I wonder if some day in the future this tradition will not go the way of animal sacrifice. (Thank god Jews don't have excommunication, or I'd probably already be a candidate.)

The next morning came, and it was showtime. We picked up the family photos from my dad and spread them around the living room. A photo of Joseph, my mom's brother, for whom my son was partially named, was there. Beryl, my father's brother for whom he is also named was not. My dad had lost all his photos in Russia, and since no one from his family survived, I never saw a photo of my paternal grandparents or anyone of my dad's brothers or sisters. My maternal grandparents were represented, as were my mom and Lisa's mom.

We gathered the things the mohel told us to provide: a clean cloth, a table, some kosher wine, a big knife (just kidding). We set up the food and drink in the dining room, as the "big event" would take place in the living room.

Lisa was distraught, and hid in the bedroom as our guests started to arrive. Frankly, it was a pretty stressful day for us both. There was trepidation in the air—an odd combination of celebration and dread. Although Lisa was upset, I felt glad to have the support of the whole community—I needed it.

The mohel arrived. My father would be holding my son for the circumcision. Did I mention my father had Parkinson's disease at the time and was prone to shaking? While I can see the humor in it now, I'm not sure if I did then. Two of my closest friends had the job of holding my father steady while he held the baby. I told my buddies if they let my father shake while he was holding the baby, it would be all over for them. They laughed of course, but nervously.

Lisa and I offered some prayers for our son, original and traditional, and we spoke directly to him for all to hear. My father spoke with eloquence and honesty, as usual. He spoke of our family members who were lost to us. He spoke of his love for me and for Lisa. He spoke of the pride he felt and of how happy he was to be alive to witness this day, although we could all see it. Tears were flowing freely all around. Then, he concluded with: "I know Lisa and Jake didn't want to know the gender of my grandchild before he was born, and I want to tell you honestly that I really didn't care if this child were a boy or girl, as long as it were healthy . . . really, honestly. But now that it turns out to be a boy. . . ." The meaning was clear, the humor apparent. The whole place cracked up. Perfect timing.

The mohel did his thing. We danced.

No kidding. I lifted my son in my arms, we made a circle, and we danced and sang. In fact, we sang, laughed, cried, and danced all at the same time. It was like some shamanistic ritual from time immemorial with the men wearing their white prayer shawls and skullcaps and the familiar songs, which affirmed our continuation as a people. We were transported to a time and place long ago in a timeless connection to our forebears. It was joyful, terrifying, uplifting, and dreadful. It was truly one of the most awe-inspiring experiences I've ever known.

"There is no intellectualizing a Bris, it takes you and shakes the very foundation of your being; it blurs the lines between corporeal existence and the mysteries of God and the spiritual world, while all the while grounding you to a people, an experience, and a depth of emotion not realized in normal space and time."

That's an excerpt from a letter I wrote to my son that night, which I intend to give to him on his eighteenth birthday. (Or maybe at his bar mitzvah. We'll see.) I guess I was pretty worked up.

The day stretched into late afternoon before everyone left. People had brought their children, their wheelchair-bound parents—it was a scene. We were spent physically and emotionally. Dovy was resting quietly in his bassinet beside our bed—it was a big day for him, too— and Lisa and I drifted off into a well-deserved sleep.

When I think back on Dovy's bris now, I think of my father speaking to everyone in my living room and how much that day meant to him. I picture my dad wrapped in his prayer shawl, supported by my closest friends, holding my son. I think of my sisters who experienced a rare breath of fresh air through Dovy's birth and got to wipe away some of the old, stale feelings of failure and hopelessness. I recall

Lisa's bravery and courage in helping my family fulfill this dream—and about the journey she'd been through. And I think of the new tiny baby that grew into the person we now know. That day, and the week preceding it, opened a new, joy-filled chapter for my family that will never be diminished or altered in my mind. I have not become any more observant of tradition than I had already been, but I'm a bit more aware of the awesome power that age-old traditions hold.

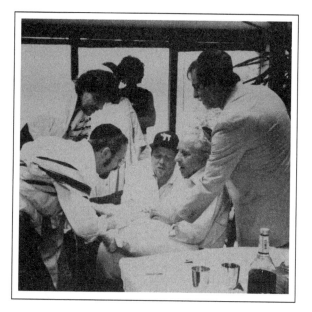

DOODY

(or Am I Really Including an Essay About That?!)

"Life is either a daring adventure or nothing."

—Helen Keller

IT'S IMPORTANT FOR CHILDREN to learn the value of keeping their word, knowing that actions have consequences, and living up to their commitments. Sometimes, as a parent, we learn that these lessons can be taught in creative ways.

My son and I (he's eleven now) were watching one of the Lord of the Rings movies the other night—*Return of the King*, the last of the great J. R. R. Tolkien trilogy. I was a great fan of the Lord of the Rings books growing up, including the first book that actually preceded the trilogy, *The Hobbit*. I was incredibly excited when the first movie, *The Fellowship of the Ring*, came out in theaters, and I went to see it right away. About halfway through the movie, I realized there was simply no way the film could possibly cover the whole story. That's when I knew there would have to be three films, one for each book in the trilogy. I was thrilled, and the films didn't disappoint. It was a great feat of movie making.

The movies are a bit violent, and some of the images, especially those of the evil armies, are disturbing. My wife and I don't like to expose our son to this type of movie very often, but I made a special case for these; presumably, because they clearly represent the triumph of good over evil—and because it's good for Dovy to be exposed to heroism and altruism and selflessness and bravery. Oh, screw it, I just thought it would be fun to watch them together.

So, Dovy and I were intently watching a pretty heavy scene in the movie. Believing that he might perish in the upcoming battle, King Theoden asks his niece for help if he were to die.

"What duty would you have me do, my Lord?" she asks.

He replies, "Duty?" as if to give himself time to ponder her question.

My son burst out in hysterical laughter.

"What could you possibly be laughing at during this very dramatic scene?" I asked, pausing the movie.

He simply looked at me as if I were an idiot. "You must be kidding," he said incredulously. "You didn't hear it?"

"Hear what?" I replied with genuine innocence.

He rewound the movie back to the offending word and played it again.

"Duty?" said King Theoden.

This time my son fell from the couch in agonizing laughter; he could hardly contain himself. He proceeded to replay this part of the movie several more times, with his hilarity barely diminishing even by the last showing.

The source of his merriment finally dawned on me. Theoden had said *duty*, which coincidentally sounded exactly like the word *doody*.

Of course, how could I have been so blind?

If you are a parent of a boy between the ages of seven and eleven (this is as far as my experience goes; perhaps it lasts well into their twenties), this information will no doubt be self-evident. The word *doody* in any way, shape, or form can always be counted on to get some laughs (much to my wife's chagrin).

Of course, *doody* is a central part of parenting, especially during the early years. And, let's face it, it's also a central part of life in general. Just think about how difficult it is to feel truly happy when you're constipated. It's hard! *Bam.* But I'm lucky. I'm actually quite regular. Every morning I have a bowel movement at 7:00 AM. Unfortunately, I don't get out of bed until 8! *Bada boom.* But seriously folks . . . I believe that no fair accounting of any person's journey would be complete without a brief jaunt in the direction of this most important subject.

It was a beautiful winter afternoon. Dovy and I were on our way for a nice brisk hike on the "heritage trail"—a lovely twenty-mile-long path that follows the route of the old train tracks as it weaves its way through local farms and forests. Lisa, Dovy, and I have enjoyed many hiking, walking, and biking adventures on that trail although this particular adventure included only Dovy and me.

We were almost out the door, but I couldn't seem to find my gloves anywhere. It was cold out, so I just grabbed my wife's brown cotton gloves that were lying on the front bench.

Dovy and I had a great walk. There's something special about an afternoon walk on a really clear winter's day, just father and son. I hadn't had enough of these with my dad. On our way back to the car, Dovy turned to me with a pained look and said, "Daddy, I really have to go."

Of course, I responded with that most dreaded question of parents everywhere: "Pee pee or doody?" I hoped it would be the former.

Dovy was about five or six years old at the time. Now, when I was that age, we stuck strictly to the number system. Number 1 was pee pee, and number 2 was, well, you know. And we never said, "I have to go." We always said, "I have to make." Don't ask me why.

My son responded, a bit desperately, "Doody."

Damn! I thought. Really, I thought *Shit!* but I couldn't bear the pun. "You think you can hold it?" I pleaded.

"No" was his emphatic response, and he had that red-faced, crunched up, semimaniacal look that told me he meant it. Plus, he was doing the "Dovy Dance"—rapidly shifting his weight from one foot to the other. That clinched it for sure—he really had to go.

Most of us have probably had this experience as a kid. Mine occurred during the second grade. I really had to go (the even number), and I somehow made it home from school but my mother wasn't home, and I was locked out of the house. I tried to hold it, I really did, but to no avail. I "made" in my pants. Not knowing what else to do, I waddled to my best friend's house and told his mom, figuring she'd let me in. Instead, she told me to go sit on my porch and wait until my mother came home. I was devastated, and I sobbed all the way home. I had professed the *ultimate* vulnerability, and I was shunned like a leper in the movie *Ben Hur*. Today, I'm a bit more understanding of her reluctance to invite me inside for a cup of hot cocoa.

I told Dovy we needed to leave the trail and go a short ways into the woods. It would be cold, but he could pull down his pants and go. I would be on the lookout for any passersby.

He hesitated slightly, but then relented. Unbelievably, neither of us had a single tissue in our pocket. I looked around for something to use as toilet tissue. All I could find were some crumply leaves, but I thought I had read somewhere that that had been banned under the Geneva Convention.

I figured it was worth the few bucks to replace the cotton gloves I was wearing, so I made an executive decision and handed him the gloves.

On the way home, Dovy and I joked about the brown gloves mixing in with the frozen brown doody. We made jokes about having a frozen penis, and I told him that the Jewish population in Alaska is called the Frozen Chosen. In other words, I tried to make the most of the situation to alleviate his embarrassment, and Dovy was more than willing to share in the laughter.

When we returned home, Lisa shouted her hello from the kitchen as we entered the house. We shouted back as we began to shed our winter clothing.

Then came the following bone-chilling words I'll never forget: "I can't find my brown *cashmere* gloves. Have either of you seen them?"

My blood froze. *Cashmere?!* I thought they were a cheap pair of fuzzy cotton gloves! (Come to think of it, Dovy had said they were really soft on his tushy.)

Dovy and I debated who would have to tell her; after all, it was *his* doody. We ended up taking the heat together. We all had a good laugh over that one . . . well, except Lisa.

My "number 2" escapades are not limited to humans. I have loved animals my whole life and had several dogs as a single young man. My first was Spanky—he lived with me at college, went with me on gigs, and lived in my different apartments in Manhattan. We were very close. As he got older, he started to develop some problems "going." He would get in position, but nothing would come out. His sweet face looked up at me in confusion.

I took him to the Animal Medical Center in Manhattan. This is one of the premier animal hospitals in the country. The vet advised me that Spanky had developed some pockets on either side of his rectum, where solid waste would get trapped. He simply couldn't push it out of those regions through his own devices. They cleaned him out and we were on our way; Spanky was clearly relieved.

Unfortunately, the situation continued, and I'd often find myself at the Animal Medical Center, where they had a twenty-four-hour emergency room. I became sort of a regular visitor there, and one vet finally suggested that I could simply do the cleanout procedure myself given the temperament of my dog. And it was simple. One would simply don latex gloves, cover a finger or two in Vaseline, place that finger in the rectum, and clean out the pockets just at the back end. Honestly, I've considered punching my own doctor in the nose for less.

Since these visits to the vet were costing me a fortune, I decided to give it a shot. Sure enough, Spanky was a trooper, and he let me do this for him. Of course, when I walked him, I'd usually try to find somewhere out of the way for us to perform our little routine.

As is often the case with German shepherds (he was actually a shepherd-Samoyed mix), Spanky developed hip dysplasia, which affected his back legs and finally his ability to walk. This had been a gradual process, but now he could barely walk. The vet suggested a very simple, low-tech, painless way to deal with the problem. I would pass a long rolled up towel under his torso, just in front of his back legs, and support his weight as he walked along on his front legs. It was surprisingly easy, and he continued to enjoy his walks. Dogs don't seem to get embarrassed, and his attitude was great.

Of course, I didn't want to tax him too much, so we stayed pretty close to home. When he became impacted and needed to be cleaned out, it became more of an issue to find an isolated spot. I finally decided to just do it wherever and whenever the urge took him. This often occurred in the evening when I had just come home from a gig and was still dressed in a tuxedo.

I'm not sure I possess the skill to accurately describe the look on people's faces as they passed us by. As a matter of fact, I'm sure I could not do it justice. Suffice it to say, if anyone ever tells you they were in the heart of Greenwich Village, minding their own business, when they came upon a young man dressed in a full tuxedo, holding a dog up by a towel, wearing white latex gloves dipped in Vaseline, bending over with a few of those fingers in the dog's backside. . . .

Believe them.

But by far the most humiliating doody story in my life took place while I was alone. Judge for yourself.

I was in the midst of building my house. I don't mean building my house as in I hired a contractor to build it. I mean literally, physically doing the work myself. I love architecture, and I love carpentry, and I love learning. Basically I bought a bunch of books, asked a lot of questions, and figured out how to design and build my house. (My wife thinks I'm Italian.)

I had purchased a lakefront property with an old summer cottage on it just about a mile from my dad's house, some sixty miles north of New York City. That was before I'd met Lisa. I tore the cottage down (all except a few walls, so it could be "grandfathered" into its current location close to the lake), and built a house in its place. As I was beginning work, my ninety-year-old neighbor came by. He asked how long I thought it would take to finish the house. I said about ten weeks. He looked deep into my eyes and said, "You'll never be finished." The jerk was right.

At the time of the incident in question, I was tearing off the old porch and framing out a wall of windows that would face the lake. I guess I should mention I had a broken leg at the time, with a cast that stretched almost up to my hip.

It was about midnight, in the dead of winter. I was alone in this freezing bungalow that had no heat or running water. I sort of lived a vagabond life in those days. I couldn't perform with the broken leg, so I had taken to working on the house by myself through all hours of day and night. I was a real recluse. Despite the cast, I could get around pretty well on crutches. In the early evening, I would order dinner from the one place that would deliver: Planet Pizza. That night, I ordered my usual—a large pie with extra cheese and loads of extra garlic (there was no one to mind), and a bottle of Coke. I also had them bring me *lots* of coffee to keep me going.

To defend myself against the cold, I was dressed in many layers, all covered by my trusty Carhartt suit. For those of you unfamiliar with the building trades, a Carhartt is a brand of workwear, which includes coverall garments that zip over street clothes, traditionally light tan and very warm. It's really a cool piece of wardrobe and always made me feel like a professional workman. And it fit right over my cast because the legs zipped up independently.

On the evening in question, the Planet Pizza "health food" diet that had sustained me thus far betrayed me. It was about midnight when the urge struck. It had begun innocently enough, with some minor stomach growling, but now it was progressing quickly. I was either having a flashback from the movie *Alien*, or I really had to go. My colon was sending emergency sirens all throughout my body, and visions of that awful day sitting on my porch in Brooklyn flooded my consciousness. I prayed to anybody's God I could think of. Given my broken leg, the lack of indoor facilities, and the numerous layers of clothing I was wearing, this could be big trouble.

Since I had no running water, my normal procedure was to do my business in the adjacent woods surrounding my house. This had been satisfactory up until then, but I'd never had an emergency like this before. I found myself woefully unprepared in my time of need.

My mad dash to make it to the woods could be more accurately described as a pitiful, hopeless gimp. And the recent snowfall didn't help the whole walking with crutches thing either. In what I consider to be one of the most impressive athletic accomplishments of my life, I actually got all the way to the woods intact. But as I desperately began the process of unzipping my Carhartt, the end came suddenly. The dynamic explosion was quick and furious, and it shook me to my core. Local wildlife in the area retreated deeper into the forest and scattered off in the moonlight in search of less odiferous pastures.

I was as alone as I had ever been.

On the edge of the woods, on this freezing, clear, moonlit winter night, broken leg, cast and all, a curious calm came over me. The worst had happened and I was still here.

I stopped the desperate attempt to remove my half-unzipped coverall, as I none-too-eagerly contemplated the task that lay ahead.

Given the lack of water and the hindrance of a full leg cast, I will leave the rest up to your imagination, or perhaps you'd just like to leave it here, and not imagine it at all. At least that's what I recommend.

At this point you might be wondering why anyone in their right mind would put a chapter like this into their book, and you'd be well within your rights to do so. I could say that these are instructive and useful stories to help people overcome their fear of looking foolish. That would be entirely true. And certainly we can agree that by airing out these extremely embarrassing stories in public, I am personally engaging in a confession that helps both to make me brave and keep me humble.

Or I can simply say my eleven-year-old son, Dovy, offered me twenty bucks if I would put a chapter in my book all about doody. Actions have consequences.

Pay up, kid.

SELF-HELP
(or I'm Okay, I'm Okay)

"The unexamined life is not worth living."

—Plato

WHAT IS OUR JOURNEY ABOUT? That's the holy work of life—to figure out what meaning there is in existence. This is the most fundamental question and the most sacred. How we get there is a decision we all need to make for ourselves. I've always been a fan of "self-help," which goes by many names and has many faces. Perhaps my interest in this came from my dad. He exemplified the do-it-yourself attitude of self-improvement. When he came to the United States, he attended night school and so excelled that the teachers begged him to attend college. He left school to get a job and support his family, but he continued his education on his own through reading—he became a self-taught expert in many things and a wise commentator on philosophy, religion, literature, culture, and world events. Whatever the influence, I became fascinated with the quest for knowledge, self-improvement, and the search for one's self.

My first true formal exposure to self-help came when an older musician friend who I respected and admired suggested I look into a program that had been valuable for him. I was about twenty at the time, and I guess he thought I could use some personal work.

I attended an informational seminar with every intention of giving this thing a shot. This was a really big deal for me because it meant I'd have to take two whole weekends off from doing gigs (and making money). The program was meant to be *experience*-based—not one of intellectualizing facts or concepts—so it was a lot of hours crammed into four very full days over two consecutive weekends.

As it turned out, the person I met with at the informational seminar *about* the program was so incredibly obnoxious that I decided I would not sign up for it after all and told him so.

His response took me off guard.

"So, you think you're smart?" he began sarcastically. "Your trusted friend suggested you try this program, and you came down here with every intention of signing up. Yet, because you don't like *my* attitude, a perfect stranger, you're willing to dump the whole thing. Do you often allow people you don't know to have that much influence over your personal decisions?"

As much as I didn't want to agree, he made a good point. Just because I thought he was a jerk, should that change what I had already decided to do? After all, my friend was also a graduate of the program, and I thought he was great. I decided to go ahead, hoping that this bozo didn't get a commission on the sale. In the end, the program turned out to be an extremely positive experience for me.

There are several *notions* I was first introduced to way back then that are still valuable and true for me today. One sticks out—the idea that we are much more than our circumstances. This is really key. During the program, participants were invited to share their personal stories—mostly about why their lives were not going the way they wanted them to. It was sort of a version of the old TV show *Queen for a Day* in which women would tell the most awful stories about their lives and the one with the worst story got to be queen for a day, complete with crown and robe and a modern appliance as a gift. (Even as a kid, I knew it was not a good sign that this was my mother's favorite TV show.)

But the people in the program I attended did not receive understanding or appliances; instead they were ridiculed. Some of the stories people shared were truly awful, and it seemed reasonable that these events could screw up your life. Yet, after each one, the leader would call the person sharing his or her story an asshole. Everyone in the room thought the leader was actually the big *asshole*! It took me a little while to get the point. If we allow the circumstances or the story of our lives to define who we are and serve as an excuse for failed lives, then we are doomed. In fact, the worse the story is, the more reasonable the excuse seems, and that's the real trap.

But there is another alternative. Think of all of those in our collective consciousness who have risen above their circumstances and written new stories for their lives. We love and revere them for it, because they show us the true nature of what is possible when we engage the human spirit. Helen Keller, Anne Frank, Steven Hawking, and Nelson Mandela are just a very few that come to mind.

I also first noticed how hung up people are in the cult of personality. Upon telling others about the program, I would often be treated to disparaging stories about the founder. But it didn't matter to me whether or not the behavior of the founder lived up to the ideals in the program. Ideas stand on their own. The world is full of the greatest notions that have come from fallible people who create something far beyond their own limitations. The founding fathers of our own country kept slaves, yet the document they created was the foundation for the eradication of slavery.

I've never looked for a personal guru to worship, but I am always looking for a good lesson or idea, which can come from anywhere and anyone. If I read a book or hear a speaker or take a lesson, I consider it a success if I come away with even one notion that has enriched my life.

Through the years, I've searched out and studied many different philosophies about life and self-improvement. I particularly like when I recognize the same concept spoken of, or taught in, different forms by different groups or people. This happens all the time. In human experience, there is nothing new under the sun. The notions I love can come from Plato or Benjamin Franklin or the Talmud or my dad, or Eckhardt Tolle, or Shirley MacLaine, or EST, or Jesus or Deepak Chopra, or *The Secret*, or Tony Robbins. Oftentimes, they are saying the same thing in different words and with different examples, but the fundamental concept remains the same. I like the title of the book *All I Really Need to Know I Learned from Watching Star Trek*. It makes me laugh and reminds me that there are lessons and metaphors everywhere.

I try to get as close to original teachings as possible so that I can divine the *original intent* as best as I can for myself. Intermediaries tend to screw things up. Unfortunately, quite often, movements that started with the best intentions get perverted by individuals who have misinterpreted the original teachings or have their own agendas. I'm quite certain Jesus Christ didn't have the crusades in mind as an outgrowth of his teachings, just as I am certain that the early communists never envisioned the different forms of totalitarianism that have risen in its name. There are innumerable instances of the same with every group or religion from Marxism to Catholicism; from Democracy to Islam to Judaism. And there is enough disagreement about original intent to go around.

I see self-help in its highest form as a journey and exploration of who we *really* are, and why we're here. It is the most holy work. Many may come up with different answers for themselves, and that is just right. There is no correct answer, and it is indeed a journey, not a destination. I believe that there are worthwhile methods and answers all around us, and I've incorporated many into my life, and continue to do so.

I imagine the most valuable part of the self-help journey would be to find a connection to the eternal part of yourself, which is connected to all things. Logistically, I believe controlling your focus, being grateful, trying to be in the moment, and interpreting events in a useful way are important components. But, most of all, not defining *who* you are solely through *what* happens to you is crucial. We are all so much more than that.

"PRETTY GOOD"
(or Looking on the Bright Side)

*"Strength does not come from physical capacity.
It comes from indomitable will."*

—Jawaharlal Nehru

O NE THING I'VE ALWAYS ADMIRED in people is the ability to change—especially having a mind that's open enough to consider a new possibility and incorporating it into one's life quickly, if it makes sense. We all know that change is not simple. New notions can often be at odds with long and deeply held beliefs, which are at the very core of how we define ourselves. Adopting new ideas means having the courage to alter those ingrained beliefs. It takes bravery to be flexible, and I've always thought, deep intelligence as well.

My dad had this wonderful quality—and for that, I consider myself fortunate. Ironically, for much of my early life, I thought of my father as a very conservative man. But there were those times, many of them in fact, that I was blessed to witness his courageous flexibility and was mature enough to recognize it.

After I moved to Manhattan in my early twenties, I would go to visit my dad in Upstate New York. I loved my dad but we quarrelled a lot when I visited. I couldn't quite remember about what—mostly lifestyle stuff I chalked up to the generation gap. But when I thought more deeply about it, I could actually remember a specific feeling that would well up in my gut just before my dad and I launched into an argument. Oddly, I couldn't recall any particular thing he said that touched this off. It was almost as if the feeling came on all by itself. I made up my mind to figure out what was causing my dad and me to argue.

Although I was paying close attention, the reason remained unclear for a long time. I knew for certain it was not my intention to argue when visiting. Yet somehow, it mostly turned out that way. Then one day, *bam!* I found it!

My father and I were having a talk, when I felt that familiar feeling begin to rise up. Before reacting to it, I stopped myself and thought, *What just happened?* That's when I found it—the trigger that got me going.

My dad made a very specific sound with his lips anytime he disapproved of something or some notion of mine. It was sort of a *tsk* sound. He had been doing this since I was a child, and, now as an adult, it made me feel like I was nine years old again.

This is not unusual. Our nervous systems sometimes make inappropriate associations between events and emotions, and, oftentimes, these triggers unconsciously drive our behavior. The most well-known illustration of this concept is Pavlov's dog. In this famous experiment by Ivan Pavlov, a bell was sounded each time the subject dogs were fed. Eventually, even without the actual presence of food, the dogs would salivate at the sound of a bell. Their nervous systems had linked the two events—a ringing bell and eating—together.

People do the same thing, only it's not always as obvious. When someone "presses our buttons," they are often triggering some deeply ingrained, long-held neurological associations. Since many of these powerful associations are developed throughout childhood, this explains why parent/child and sibling relationships often have a very unique quality—the ability to set each other off with even the most subtle of behaviors, as in this case with my dad.

Usually, with my dad, I would just get defensive about whatever we were discussing, and dig in, and we'd argue. In this instance, I kept my feelings in check, and we avoided a confrontation.

I tested my theory again to be certain. Sure enough, like clockwork, anytime my dad would make that sound, anger welled up in me. Emotionally, I was thrust back to my childhood, and I could *feel* the shame of my father's disapproval.

The next time it happened, I brought it up.

"That's it!" I interrupted. "Don't do that anymore!"

My dad was taken aback. "Do what?" he asked, somewhat bewildered.

"Make that sound!" I said.

"What sound?" he replied.

"That *tsk* sound you make with your lips when you don't agree with what I'm saying. It's very condescending."

"What in the world are you talking about?" he exclaimed.

I copied the sound as best as I could to show him, and I explained how he used to make that sound when I was a kid and had done or said something he didn't approve of. "Every time you make that sound, Dad, it makes me feel like I'm a child, which I'm not. I get angry, and we end up arguing."

He responded in Yiddish. *"Du bist meshige?"* (Are you crazy?) My father always spoke in Yiddish when he felt vulnerable.

"Look, it's very clear," I said. "My nervous system links your *tsk* sound to a feeling of childhood disapproval from you. Then I get defensive and pissed off."

Then he made the *tsk* sound again!

"Dad! Don't make that sound!"

"This is a *meshigas!*" he bellowed. (A craziness!) "It's time to grow up!"

That's all I needed. *It's time to grow up* was another of my dad's favorite sayings that made me feel like an infant. *One battle at a time,* I reminded myself.

I decided to take a different approach.

"Dad, do you love me?" I asked.

"Don't be a baby," he said in his best real-men-don't-show-love manner—also carried over from my childhood days. Yet, I could see this new direction caught him off guard, and I pressed the issue.

"Dad, It's a simple question, just answer yes or no. Do you love me?" I repeated.

"Oh, this is ridiculous," he said exasperatedly.

"Dad!"

"Yes, of course I love you!"

At the time, I couldn't remember ever hearing those words so directly from him. But rather than make a huge deal over it, I stayed on point.

"Fine," I replied. "I figure we have two choices, I could go into therapy for about ten years, and I'm sure I'll get over the whole *tsk* thing. Or . . . we could all save ourselves a lot of time and money if you could simply stop making that sound. Since I'm your son and you love me, could you do that for me?"

"This is unbelievable!" he said, storming into the other room.

My father never made that sound in front of me again.

Another such time was near the end of my dad's life. He was eighty-four years old and suffering from intense Parkinson's disease. Fortunately, it did not affect his brain, just his physical body. He was in lots of pain almost all of the time, and suffered from, among other ailments, something called restless leg syndrome (RLS), a particularly insidious and continuous involuntary movement of his legs.

I was in the process of writing my show "A Jew Grows in Brooklyn," and I had adopted the habit of walking/jogging six miles every morning around the country roads near my home in Upstate New York, where I'd moved some years before to be closer to my dad when he fell ill. I would take a route that brought me by his house, and I'd always stop in for my morning visit.

The morning in question, I walked in as usual, with my standard "How ya doin', Pop?"

I was taken aback by a response I'd never heard from him before: "My life is miserable," he mumbled, his heavily accented English barely audible.

I became deeply concerned, because I knew that what we believe to be true about our lives directly affects our well-being and that the words we choose to describe our existence have a powerful influence on our actual reality. This is, of course, true in both a positive and negative sense. In this case, I firmly believed that my dad's adoption of the belief that his life was miserable would hasten his illness. I had faith that he could improve his outlook and his health, or at least his mental health, by focusing on the things he had to be grateful for and dwelling less on the negatives.

Of course, that is easier said than done when someone is in pain, yet true nonetheless. How would I impart this information to my eighty-four-year-old ailing father? Was I about to start lecturing my dad on how to live, how to think? Would I tell him how he *should* feel about his pain and circumstances?

Instead, I tried to be cheery in the face of his statement. I told him I understood and that hopefully things would look up. After all, we were trying all sorts of treatments, both conventional and alternative, to improve his quality of life.

Still, over the next few weeks, the "my life is miserable" response became more and more prevalent. If I let him wallow in that state, I knew he would quickly deteriorate, and we would soon lose him. We had a history of honesty, so I decided to take a chance.

The next day when I stopped in and said, "How ya doin', Pop?" and I got the same troubling response, "My life is miserable," I went for it . . . big time.

"Dad, I can't come here and listen to bullshit. Sure, I know you're in pain, but you also have so much to be thankful for. You have a roof over your head, and you don't have to worry about where your next meal is coming from. You have a wonderful wife who loves you, a son who visits you *every* day, a daughter-in-law and a grandson who love you so much. The community reveres you. If your life is miserable, what about some Holocaust survivor who is living in a cold water flat in the Bronx, with no family, all alone and is eating dog food from a tin?"

"Who are *you* to tell me what I should feel?!" he responded with great ire. "You have no idea what it's like to be in this pain. You have some nerve coming and telling me this . . . you're just a *pisher*." (Meaning a child.)

Well, a heated argument ensued. I had not seen my dad this angry for many years.

"I love you!" I shouted. "That's why I'm telling you this! If you continue this way, you'll get sicker and die! Don't be so selfish! Think about your grandson; don't pity yourself so much!" Tears were streaming from our eyes and our voices were at top volume. My dad's second wife, Ruth, was screaming at me to leave: "He'll have a heart attack and die right there!"

To be honest, the thought had crossed my mind that this argument was too much for him to handle in his frail state. I was taking a huge risk, and it was *not* going well. So I lowered my voice, and we both calmed down a bit. I explained again how much I loved him and that I used my harsh words because I loved him. "I'll be back tomorrow, Pop," I told him and kissed him on the forehead. He softened a bit, but I could still feel the anger. "Get some rest," I said, and left.

I was on edge the rest of the day. *What if he was too weak to survive such a blow?* It would be almost as if I had killed him, and I would carry that burden with me for as long as I lived. I could easily have left him to his own methods of dealing with his problems and not so aggressively tried to impart upon him my theory of life, a theory some might even find foolish.

I tossed and turned all night long, the argument dominating my thoughts, replaying it over and over again. The next morning, as I nervously walked to my dad's house, I could think of nothing else.

Upon reaching the door, I held my breath and entered.

I tried to be as nonchalant as possible and said my usual, "How ya doin', Pop?"

My dad looked at me with a huge grin on his face—the biggest I'd seen in a long, long time, and replied, "Pretty good."

The hug I gave my dad that morning was the greatest ever. From that morning on, and for the next few years, despite the obvious progression of his illness, Dad's response to "How ya doin, Pop?" was always the same: "Pretty good."

I'll never forget nor underestimate the courage required to make the transition of spirit that my father went through. I take great

pride in the fact that he shared with me his belief that our conversation that day had elongated his life; and in fact, he did have a rebirth of sorts, notwithstanding the worsening of the disease's physical aspects.

As an added bonus, I am sure that my father's behavior toward the end of his life, of which this story is indicative, was one of the most valuable lessons he gave to my son, his grandson. I hope it will stay with him throughout his life. I also hope that, when my time comes, I can be as courageous and heroic, and as flexible in my heart as my dad was—and remained in his final years.

AUTHOR'S NOTE: *I am enormously proud of the hard work I put into my relationship with my dad. It takes great courage for a child to approach a parent as honestly as I did my father. But it also takes an enlightened and flexible parent to adopt ideas that seem foreign to them and challenge their view of the world. I am so proud of my dad and so fortunate to have had him.*

I've mentioned these and other stories to adult friends of mine who are having challenges with their parents. I remind them that their parents love them, and most parents would do anything for their children; sometimes they just need a little nudge. Being vulnerable and honest can bring out the protective qualities they might have buried long ago. I also remind them that time is short.

Unfortunately, many friends respond by saying things like, "Well, you don't know my dad," or "It's great that works for you, but it wouldn't with my folks."

In my heart, I suspect many of them might be surprised if they tried.

FEAR

(or The Worst-Case Scenario)

*"A ship in the harbor is safe, but that is
not what ships are built for."*

—John A. Shedd

FEAR IS ARGUABLY THE MOST IMPORTANT and fundamental challenge we face in life. It can paralyze us to the degree that all else is undoable. Picture the person who falls in a movie when being chased by the monster. For goodness sake, *get up and run!* They can't, even to save themselves, because they are paralyzed by fear.

Many of us go to great lengths rationalizing why we don't do this or that . . . when in fact, the root cause for many of our decisions is fear. It's nothing to be ashamed of—it's part of our fundamental journey. But letting fear run our life and allowing it be the primary motivator for the decisions we make—consciously or not—is the major stumbling block to leading a happy and fulfilled life.

I sometimes joke with Lisa that I'm probably the bravest person she's ever known, because I have so much internal fear that it's an enormous effort for me to do even the simplest things. And I'm only half kidding. I often imagine the worst possible things happening to those dearest to me, and I fight hard to ward off those visions. It's a colossal challenge for me not to overprotect or smother my son or, for that matter, my wife.

What works for me is to allow the visions to exist as real possibilities instead of denying them. If my mind imagines a car on the other side of the road leaving its lane and hitting us head on, it doesn't help me to think that's just a silly thought. In fact, it *is* one of an infinite number of *real* possibilities. What helps me is to acknowledge that it exists, but also that it is extremely unlikely. That is the truth, and my brain knows it. Denying disastrous possibilities doesn't make them go away. Since it's also true that we attract the things we focus on, remembering that helps me to have the strength to alter my focus away from my fear as well.

I think I learned not to deny disastrous possibilities from the history of my people in Eastern Europe and elsewhere during World War II. They reasonably refused to believe the reports that Jews were being sent to gas chambers in a systematic effort of mass murder. This notion was understandably unbelievable in the 1940s days of Glenn Miller and modern civilized society, but true nonetheless. Just because something is unlikely or unbelievable doesn't mean it's not possible.

The above may seem absurd, but I don't view it as particularly unreasonable that I have these internal thoughts and feelings. I'm clear that growing up in the shadow of the Holocaust has taken its toll on my psyche. And yet, I have learned to live my life in joy and beauty and gratitude. By most measures, I have lived a life not typical of a fearful person. Each one of us is capable of this—it is our birthright.

September 11, 2001 caused me to examine my internal fear anew. After 9/11, there was much talk in the media about how the event shattered people's previous sense of personal security. My immediate reaction to these comments was visceral. I'd *never* felt secure. I was *always* aware, somewhere deep inside, that the nature of our civilization is fragile and temporal—and that at any moment the "knock" could come at the door and all the agreements we live by could disappear. Of course, I use the term "knock" metaphorically, but the Holocaust—where the "knock" was not a metaphor, but a reality—defines a part of who I am and how I think. That's fine. We all need to take what we are given and make a successful life out of it. No excuses. But while my own fear was no doubt influenced by my family's experience, it's also true that the fragility of the human condition exists without the Holocaust or 9/11 or any number of other catastrophes. The human journey is filled with fear. Learning to control, embrace, manage, and harness that fear is part of our lesson on earth. Call it what you will, it is part of our process.

There is a wonderful movie that I have watched with my family many times. It is called *Defending Your Life*, and it stars Albert Brooks and Meryl Streep. It is a funny and touching movie, but what makes it so interesting to me is its core concept. The Albert Brooks character dies early in the movie and goes to a sort of "waiting station" where he literally ends up defending his life. In a courtroom setting, they replay chosen scenes from his life, but he is not defending his actions as right or wrong, simply determining whether they were motivated by fear. The point being that if you had successfully learned how to overcome fear as the motivating factor in your life, you moved on to the next "level" of existence. If, on the other hand, it was shown that fear controlled your decisions, you would be sent back to earth for another lifetime to learn to handle fear.

Many successful people talk about their fears, and heroes talk about how frightened they were in battle. It is natural, but those people successfully put fear into its proper place. Focusing too much on fear only begets more fear. If we focus on something larger than ourselves, we can displace fear. Finding a faith that supports our true self, that everlasting part of our being or soul, that thing in us that transcends this life, can be very useful in controlling or dispelling fear. I don't mean any faith in particular. The key is to not let fear run—or more accurately, *ruin*—your life.

I'm afraid my sisters were casualties of lives where fear reigned: fear of failure, fear of success, fear of taking chances, fear of being different, fear of playing the fool.

Do I still have fears? I do. And yet, I am an extremely optimistic person and live primarily in joy. I simply do not let my fears stand in my way. Nor do I let them control my life. Nor do I let them keep me in a state that will cause illness. When asked, my advice is to control your focus, live in gratitude, get in touch with your true self, keep working, and keep loving—whatever it takes. We alone are responsible for our journey—no crutches—not fear, not our circumstances, not our parents, not our past.

And yet, I have a confession to make about a small comical concession I've made to my internal fears. This is something I show to my friends to get a laugh. Before I unveil my treasure, I say, "Hey, you want to get a glimpse into my madness?" (I'm still only half kidding.)

I have an early Macintosh computer in my upstairs closet at home. It's the kind that looks like a white plastic-coated metal box with a small screen. How old is it? Well, years ago, I called tech support to find out why I was having trouble getting on the Internet. When the representative asked me to check how much RAM I had, I said, "Four megabytes."

The guy cracked up and told me I was lucky I'd ever gotten on the Internet.

I keep this computer for one reason.

If civilization ever goes mad again, I will have a computer at my disposal that was probably manufactured before the top-secret encrypting of all computers went into effect and therefore cannot be controlled by unfriendly outside forces. I can deliver it to the resistance to help in their fight that ultimately saves humankind. And I figure there's probably a guy in Australia (where, by the way, lots of Holocaust survivors went and had kids, too) doing the same thing I'm doing right about now. When the trouble starts, someone will tell someone, who will tell someone else, who will have heard of me and my *fakakte* computer, and we'll help save the world (me and the guy in Australia).

Welcome to my world.

MY STAGE SHOW
(or The How Takes Care of Itself)

"The future has several names. For the weak,
it is impossible. For the faint hearted, it is unknown.
For the thoughtful and valiant, it is ideal."

—Victor Hugo

REGARDLESS OF HOW MUCH PERSONAL WORK we do on ourselves, there are always new doors to open and new journeys to embark upon. That's the fun part—and also the *scary* part. The unknown in life always has that mix of opportunity and challenge—sort of like venturing into a dark patch of forest. It's great when we finally reach a place in our lives where anticipation and excitement outweigh any doubt, and we can use our inner perspective and joy to light the way through the uncertainty.

When I decided to write my stage show, it was not out of desperation, but out of love. I had a desire to make the most of what I'd been given in life and do something worthwhile with it. Telling the story of my family in a way that brought joy and hope and education to people was what I settled on.

I knew I'd have to make use of all my emotional resources to succeed. This would be a huge undertaking. I was still giving people pleasure through music—mostly at private events—and was making a good living at it. Taking a leap of faith with the show would require risking the security I'd established. Although I was happy spending lots of time with my wife and son, I knew deep inside I was not burning the candle as brightly as I might and not making the best use of the gifts I'd been given. Dovy was in school now, and I wasn't getting any younger, so I felt that if I were ever going to take a chance and really go for it, this was the time. I discussed the situation with Lisa, and thank God, I married the right person. She supported whatever I thought I needed to do.

The first thing I did was to spend two hours alone every single day, rain or shine, snow or sleet, walking the country roads near my home. This time was spent listening to self-help tapes and thinking and getting myself in great physical condition. I would spend another hour or so doing visualization exercises designed to find out who I really was and what I really wanted.

While this may seem like a waste of time in preparation for writing a stage show, having a clear direction is actually the most important part of any process. I was figuring out what specific results I really wanted to achieve and *why I wanted those results*. I knew from my past experience that figuring out the *what* and especially the *why* of a goal was absolutely critical. There are innumerable ways to be successful in any enterprise. Some things work and others don't, but having a clear vision and powerful reasons behind what you do gives you the tenacity necessary to keep going when the going gets tough. When you know the *what* and the *why*, the *how* takes care of itself. You're bound to hit many traffic jams along the way, but having a clear destination and purpose can keep you on track to the finish line.

Here's a good example of what I mean. I had planned a night out for me and Lisa at a really fancy restaurant. I wanted to make Lisa feel loved and appreciated. While we were getting ready to leave, I noticed the front hallway table was covered with unopened mail (my bad). This is a big point of contention between us, and I realized that if my goal were truly to make Lisa feel loved and appreciated, I could accomplish that more effectively (and more economically) by simply clearing the mail off the table. Notwithstanding her love of great restaurants, Lisa emphatically agreed.

If you're wondering, we went to dinner, too.

I began developing my show with an evening to honor my father in the community. He was ill and running out of time, and I thought it best to honor him while he was alive instead of posthumously. I sang some songs, showed some slides of my dad's life, and told some funny stories. The show was a huge success, and my father was truly honored. But I knew I had something special when my friend Warren—a very successful Broadway musician—approached me after the performance.

Warren is very funny, and he can be quite dry. He took me aside and gave me his critique of the evening. "Hey, Jake, this show sucks less than a lot of other stuff I've seen." This was truly high praise from Warren, and I felt encouraged to further develop this concept.

I was pleased I had made a good start. Then I worked my butt off. There were many challenges along the way, but I continued to keep my eye on the goal and to stay open to mentoring and experimentation. I kept other very important concepts in mind as well.

First, I asked good questions. When something went wrong, I never asked myself or others, "Why is this happening to us?" I would always ask, "How can this work for us, and what can we learn from this?" Asking good questions leads to better answers.

I also controlled my focus. While it is extremely important to anticipate possible obstacles, focusing too much energy on what may go wrong can paralyze the entire effort. I kept my sights set on the goal. My ideas worked, and the show became a huge success as I outline in "Setting the Stage" at the beginning of this book, but success brings with it its own new set of challenges.

How do you do a show night after night for years and keep it fresh? I experimented and searched for deeper understanding of the piece and myself as we continued to run. I found that the less I thought of myself and the more I thought of the audience, the easier it was to stay focused. And, although it seems contradictory, I also learned that I always needed to have a good time for myself while I was onstage and stay open and flexible. That sometimes led to interesting situations.

During one performance I had been told there would be a woman in the audience who was celebrating her ninety-fifth birthday. I found out where she would be seated, and when I had the opportunity, I introduced her to a nice round of applause. She seemed pretty "with it," so from up onstage, I asked her for her secret to longevity and health.

"The three P's," she replied forcefully.

"What are the three P's?" I asked innocently.

With a totally straight face, she replied, "No pets . . . no plants . . . no penises."

The thunderous laughter from the audience is still clear in my mind—but what really scared me was my wife's question to this woman in the lobby after the show. "Why no plants?" she asked.

Yikes! Did Lisa really think it was reasonable to avoid pets and penises?

The response she received was carefully thought out and wryly delivered, "I don't want anything I have to take care of."

At another performance, while repeating what my father's business associates had told me at my bar mitzvah, I said my line, "Be like your father—your father is an honest man." A gentleman in the front row shouted out loud enough for the entire audience to hear, "An honest man, a smart man. Your father was a wonderful man!"

The audience laughed at this lighthearted interruption, and so did I.

When the laughter died down, I said, "Who are you?"

"I was at your bar mitzvah!" he responded proudly.

After every show, I meet with audience members in the lobby. I've heard so many stories from so many people who somehow knew my father and that always touches me deeply—but a few stand out among the others.

On one occasion, a couple in maybe their late seventies approached me after waiting patiently in line to speak with me. As the gentleman began to open his mouth to speak, his wife elbowed him in the side and said, "Tell him!"

He hadn't gotten a word out yet. He turned to her, and said, "Let me say hello, then I'll tell him." He turned again to address me.

"Tell him now!" she said, more insistently this time.

As he turned back to address her again, I butted in. (The waiting line was long.)

"Perhaps you should just tell me," I said.

The husband and I shared a knowing smile.

"Okay. I'll tell him," he told her and proceeded to tell me the story about how he and his wife went to my father's store for some furniture. As it turned out, my dad didn't carry the pieces they were looking for, but he called a friend who did. The young couple was very happy with both the furniture and the price. A few months later, they received a letter and a check in the mail from my father. The store owner where they'd purchased the furniture had sent my father a commission for the referral. It wasn't my dad's intention to earn commission on the sale so he sent the money to the couple.

"Do you understand what that means?!" the wife shouted at me. This was clearly the moment she'd been waiting for: "We would have never known that he got that money . . . ever! Do you know who does a thing like that? Do you know who? Your father, that's who! *That's* the kind of person your father was!"

They'd been telling that story to friends and family for forty-five years. It seemed we had come full circle. The show began with a dedication to my father, and now that he was gone, I was still hearing about him.

Of course, my father was a very central figure in my life, and when performing the show in New York, I often stopped by his house before leaving for the city. We'd been fortunate to have garnered so many good reviews for the show, and I would dutifully bring them home for my dad to read. Yet, no matter how good they were, or the importance of the source, he never seemed to get too excited about them, which always disappointed me a bit, but I never mentioned it. Then one day I brought him one of the many letters I'd received from regular folks who had attended the show.

He simply exploded with pride and excitement. "This is something!" he raved. He looked at me a bit calmer now. "Don't get me wrong," he said. "Good reviews are nice, but reviewing shows is what those people do for a living." Then he paused and got excited again. "But when the *people* speak, that's something to be proud of!"

Seeing the excitement on my dad's face and hearing his voice—and knowing how many letters like the one I showed him I've received—made me know for sure that my plan had worked. Although I never could have predicted the details of "how" we got where we did, I know that thinking through the "what" and the "why" helped me achieve my goal of spreading hope and love and joy and education—and connecting with people the way I had intended.

BACK TO BROOKLYN
(or A Bond That Will Never Fade)

"Our life is what our thoughts make it."

—Marcus Aurelius Antoninus

SOMETIMES WHEN WE RETURN to a place we've known after a long journey, we can see it with new eyes. When it came to returning to Brooklyn, I saw that things I thought were true were no longer so, nor had they ever really been. It's funny how we sometimes live under the impression that something is true, but it turns out later we were mistaken. When you accept something as true, all the attendant feelings and emotions that go along with that belief become real—even when the underlying belief is false. For instance, let's say you heard through the grapevine that a good friend of yours called you "a swine." You'd be hurt and upset, and maybe angry, and experience all the emotions that would accompany that belief and those feelings. Now, it's two weeks later, you find out that the party who'd repeated this to you didn't have a hearing aid in, and it turns out your friend actually called you "divine." That's a huge difference, and the feelings associated with those two beliefs are very different. However, the hurt and pain you felt were still as real as if you had actually been called a swine. That was your reality. What makes all the difference is what you *think* happened and what you adopted as true. Not what *really* happened.

I was recently surprised to learn that much of what I thought and felt as a child about being different was really only in my head—especially as it related to the perception of me by my friends. I got a valuable and pleasurable glimpse at this when I recently had the chance to hook up with a group of my old friends in our old Brooklyn neighborhood. Going back there revealed some true surprises, and it was a great day, too.

I was so excited to see my old childhood friends, some of whom I hadn't seen for forty years. Being in the confines of our old neighborhood with them added another emotional layer to the already hugely anticipated day. We were getting together to talk about the old days for a documentary based on my stage show "A Jew Grows in Brooklyn." I spent the early part of the day with my old "best friend," Andy Levine, just walking around my block and the places we knew. My house was altered, but not so much. The white picket fence my father and I built (against my will) was gone, as was his flower garden. But the man who lived there still remembered it, and he even remembered my playing drums in the back room when he originally came to look at the house. The Chinese Lots seemed so much smaller than I remembered it, but I did notice a few broken windows, so I guess times haven't changed all that much. The grocery store where I used to work still had the same smell. I closed my eyes, took a deep breath, and I went back to a time when I delivered groceries by bike for a quarter and sometimes got a dime tip. I passed by the former site of La Croce Via, where I'd learned so much from my friend Joe.

The synagogue on Remsen Avenue, where I'd first sang in the choir, was still there. It's being used as a church now, and I took great comfort in knowing that the community still gathered there as we did many years before (ironically, all the Hebrew writing and Jewish stars remain on the facade). I strolled down my block where we'd played punchball and stickball, and if I closed my eyes, I could almost hear my mom calling, *"Yohnkeeee!"* from our front porch.

This was where I grew up, this was my life, and it felt familiar and welcoming. In fact, everything was pretty much the same—only the names and faces had changed. I was pleasantly surprised that the neighborhood hadn't fallen into decay, like my old haunts in the Catskills, where things were broken down and in disarray. East Flatbush was beautiful and full of life. I found it ironic that the neighborhood was mostly occupied by immigrant families, whose American-born kids had funny-sounding names, too. I wonder if those kids struggle with "not fitting in" the way I did.

I thoroughly enjoyed my visit to the old neighborhood, but the most exciting part of the day was simply being with my old friends. We met at our old haunt, Ditmas Park, and we each showed up individually. Each time a new friend would arrive, we'd hug, laugh, kid, and holler, using old nicknames many of us hadn't heard in years. They all knew me as Yonkee, and boy did that feel *great!*

Old, warm feelings of our childhood came rushing back as we caroused in the outfield where we'd played baseball and shared old photographs on the benches across from the basketball courts. Some of us even got in a short "run" with some local kids who were impressed that we "still had game," and we joked they should have an ambulance standing by just in case we keeled over.

The group of us finally ended up parking ourselves on the concrete handball courts where we used to play so that we could "comfortably" reminisce. We hardly noticed that the cameras had been rolling the entire time. We were all too busy being back in the old neighborhood with the gang to be aware of much else than each other at this point.

I mentioned how different I'd felt from the other kids, with my un-American Yiddish name and being the child of Holocaust survivors—and how all I wanted was to just fit in. (You know *that's* been one of the main themes of my life.) To my everlasting surprise, none of my friends remembered me as being any different and they all thought "Yonkee" was cool. I was shocked! Although I'd worked so hard to fit in, somehow I still thought that I was different and that everyone knew it.

As it turns out, all my friends had been way too involved in their own adolescent troubles to pay much attention to mine. It seemed we had more in common than I imagined. Everyone had "family secrets" of their own. David's family was on welfare, but hid it. Andy's father was agoraphobic, and when Linda's parents got divorced, she was so ashamed, she told everyone her dad was a traveling salesman. Karen related how she'd almost been molested by our friend's father when she was at his home. She never found out what was going on in that house, but our friend who lived there later committed suicide. I didn't know any of this growing up, and it seemed my delusions of being so different were of my own making. But what we perceive to be true *is* true for us—and that was true for me.

Jeff talked about how as a boy he couldn't understand why he'd be beaten for talking to his brother at night when it was time for bed. In fact, I learned that almost every one of my friends got hit by their parents when they got in trouble. I was truly surprised. I had always thought my parents used this form of discipline because it was their way of life in Europe. Turns out we were, again, not so dif ferent after all.

I even discovered that one of my friend's parents were also Holocaust survivors. I'd had no idea. We'd certainly never spoken about it or acknowledged our unique bond. I was struck by the similarity of our childhood experiences, and my friend and I talked at length.

I was beginning to realize how skewed my perception of things had been. I actually felt a little sorry for the kid I was who was so desperate for inclusion and "normalcy"—when no one around me had it either. I could almost feel my young self close at hand, being in our old park, and I wanted to hug him and tell him it was okay.

One friend shared that he recently got a divorce and was accused by his wife of wanting their life to be like *The Donna Reed Show*. He said, "Is that so wrong? We all wanted that." It seemed we were all different, and everybody wanted to fit in.

We held on to each other tight as friends in those early days, yet we'd never previously discussed any of our "secrets." Some thought that simply having those secrets, though unspoken, made us feel even closer as kids. We were all just happy to gather in the street or the schoolyard or the park to play—to escape our homes and our families for at least a little while—and have the simple unspoken support of our friends.

That day made me think of *all* my old friends and who we'd become. Our inner-city, lower-middle-class Brooklyn neighborhood has spawned all types of adults. We are lawyers and doctors, gay and straight, gamblers and scientists, divorced and happily married, well adjusted and maladjusted, drug addicts and entertainers. We have died of AIDS, illness, violence, in war, and by our own hand.

The names and faces and details of our lives may be different, but the fundamental challenges we face are most often more alike than not. We were more similar than I might have imagined—and that is true for most people.

Ultimately, we are all of us travelers on the same road, headed toward the same destination. I've spent the last years telling my family story on the stage, and now in a book. It resonates with people because wherever they're from and whatever the details of their circumstances, we all recognize and experience the same human qualities: courage and honesty, fear and isolation, illness and death, and hope and rebirth.

My personal journey does not end here, as none of ours do until we take our last measured breath. We continue our voyage of discovery in our lives every day. If days are pages in a book, we are free to write on them what we would have our chapters say and have our legacy be.

That day in Brooklyn, my friends and I felt a special bond for each other—one that time had not diminished. We had cared for each other as children, and it was beautiful to experience the sincere affection that still remained. We were, as we all are, more alike than we imagine.

It seems that in being different, I had finally fit in after all.

EXIT, STAGE LEFT
(or the Journey Is the Destination)

"Love is all you need."

—John Lennon

SO, IT SEEMS I'VE FINALLY COME to the end of this "chapter" of my life—thank you for joining me. I hope some of the notions that have helped me over the years have been useful for you as well, and that perhaps you've even recalled some events from your own life you may have temporarily forgotten. For me, this journey has once again amazed and confirmed how each new adventure challenges us to reach higher.

Writing the book has dared me to make use of many of the life concepts that I espouse under challenging circumstances. Since I was juggling so many projects and responsibilities at once, it turned into a period of many eighteen-hour workdays (and nights—you should be able to tell those chapters that were written at 4:00 AM!). It would have been easy to totally lose sight of the journey and the big picture without those ideas to rely upon. In fact, some important things did fall by the wayside—for instance, I find myself twelve pounds heavier now than when I began (with the challenge to drop it so I can get

236

into my costumes when the show goes back up in a matter of weeks!). But I'm pleased because I tried to be my best—not perfect—just my best, and I learned so much in the process. I trust reading it didn't put on any pounds for you.

Today I went out in a huge snowstorm (eighteen inches already) with Lisa and Dovy, and we got really silly—I'm so grateful for that. Yet also today, a man died when a tree fell on him in Central Park under the weight of that same snow. I'm fairly certain he had no idea this would be his last day on earth. I know there is a huge lesson there, and it's a stark reminder yet again to be present and grateful for each moment. As goal oriented as we might be, let us try to remember that the journey is the destination, and that we can choose to be joyful right now.

I am so excited and looking forward to actually meeting all of you who have read the book and talking to you about your thoughts and feelings—just as with my show. My experiences gain new importance for me when I know they've affected others in some way. Conversations are alive, and I hope that the book has been a conversation between us. I'll know when I'm out there meeting you.

There is an old story in the Jewish tradition of a man who asked for all the teachings to be explained to him while standing on one foot. Rabbi Hillel responded: "What is hateful to you, do not do to your neighbor. The rest is commentary." And in fact, the Golden Rule of "do unto others" has been prevalent in various cultures throughout the world for centuries.

I'm pleased that wise people have had such a simple solution to life as the one above, because although I sometimes wish I had something more profound to say—if asked the same question, I would simply respond, "It's all about love. The rest is commentary."

Thanks for the company—I hope to meet you someday at a book signing or at the show. Until then, as my friend Deepak Chopra says, I'll meet you in the field of all possibilities.

With love,

ACKNOWLEDGMENTS

"It's in a state of gratitude that fear
flees and abundance reigns."

—Anthony Robbins

WRITING THIS BOOK has been a labor of love and a much more daunting process than I would have ever imagined. I am so fortunate to have the loving and expert guidance of my fabulous editor, Carol Rosenberg, on my journey. From the 2:00-AM editing sessions, to putting up with my constant desire to do my best (which led to A LOT of late changes), Carol was always in good humor (well, almost always) and unfailingly willing to go the extra mile. I am deeply in her debt and to her husband, Gary, as well for allowing the madness of the last several weeks. And also to the rest of the crew at HCI, especially the fabulous Kim Weiss in publicity, the irrepressible Tonya Woodworth in editorial, and the tireless art director Larissa Hise Henoch and her staff. My deepest gratitude also to the publisher, Peter Vegso, for inviting me into his family.

I've been blessed with friends and confidants without whom much of what I've accomplished over the last few years, including this book, would not have been possible. My two best men, Avi Hoffman and Dan Denerstein, who I know I can always count on for support of any type at any time, and also our dear friend Pat Phillips. My original director and documentary filmmaker Jon Huberth, who has become a trusted and valued friend. My great production stage manager Jeff Stevenson and my original New York musical director Elysa Sunshine. And one of my oldest childhood friends who has also become one of my newest and most valued advisors, and who really has my back, Andrew Levine.

There are others who have stepped up to help me out of the goodness of their hearts—literary agent Mollie Glick, authors Dick Wiley, John Thorn, Scott Benarde, and Dick Kalish, and my friend Abby Koffler, who introduced me to my great theatrical agent Scott Morris at ICM. And there are kind and talented people like Jay Kholos, who advised me about the name of the show so early on, and Michael Chomet, who is slaving away editing the documentary as this is being written.

I have a special place in my heart for those who believed in me and took a chance on investing in my show when it was just a pipe dream—thanks to Barry Lewis, Scott Rosmarin, Harry Waiser, Kevin Lesser, and Seth Pulver—and their families. And to my two producing partners who came on board in New York, Dana Matthow and Phil Roger Roy.

I've made use of so many teachings available and have so many enlightened souls to thank—but I think the person I depended on most to keep me going during my original creation of the show (even though we've never met) was peak performance coach Anthony Robbins, through his many books, tapes, and programs.

Of course, as with everything my greatest support is my wife,

Lisa, the smartest, most creative and grounded person I know—without whom I would not be able to do any of what I do. And also my greatest inspiration—our son, Dovy, the love of our lives—without whom nothing would have the same meaning.

A NOTE FROM
THE DIRECTOR OF THE SHOW
(or Picture Postcard Memories
of My Journey with Jake)

JAKE IS MY FRIEND AND NEIGHBOR. He called me up one early spring day in 2005.

"Aren't you some sort of theatre person? Don't you direct or something? Something . . . like that?"

I'd known Jake and Lisa for well over a decade, been to their wedding and the baby shower, but was spared Dovy's briss.

"Yes, Jake, even though I make films, my real training is in theatre. I actually have my MFA in directing from the Yale Drama School."

"Really? Wow! That's great! You can direct my show!"

"Show? What show?"

And so it began. Jake told me he was expanding his birthday tribute to his father, Jonah. "And I'm making it into a show with music and taking it to Broadway. Come over. I'll show you what I have."

I got in my canoe and made the fifteen-minute paddle to Jake's house on the other side of Round Lake. I was thinking this whole thing smacked of an old Mickey Rooney/Judy Garland movie. "You have seventeen pairs of tap shoes and I have a barn! Let's put on a show!" Broadway. Who was he kidding? But I was willing to humor him. And it was a nice day for a paddle.

We spent a couple of hours on Jake's deck. He partly acted, partly sang, partly told me the show he then called *Growing Up in America*. I was enchanted. But I told him he really needed a director who had New York connections, was still active in the business, and could be more of a help. And I paddled home.

Two weeks later Jake called me again.

"I've talked to a bunch of directors, and they're good and all that. But you are the person I trust. You have to direct the show for me."

What could I say? Jake didn't give me choice. He wasn't asking me to direct the show now. He was telling me I was directing the show. So, I guess I was directing the show.

This was my first brush with what I now assume was his father, Jonah's, influence on Jake. Jake had gotten to the point in his life where trust and instinct, loyalty and friendship guided him and the choice of who he wanted to be associated with and how he wanted to live his life. You talked, you came to an agreement, you shook hands, you went to work. Volumes of legal documents can never take the place of your "word." It was Gem Upholstery all over again. Nothing is so liberating in any creative endeavor—probably any endeavor—as going into it with this feeling of trust and respect.

A week into rehearsals, Jake is driving us into the city, and I'm on the phone with my film partner. "It's this one-person show, but it's really more, because there's this four-person band on stage, and there will be projections and singing and Yiddish lullabies and rock-'n'-roll and drum solos, and it's about the Holocaust and the Catskills and Brooklyn and the search for identity."

There was stunned silence on the other end of the line. My description did sound ridiculous, I'll admit, but that was really the show!

"*Well, who are you doing this with?*"

"*Some Jew,*" I said. (Jake and I were always irreverent like that with each other.)

"*A Jew from Brooklyn?*" He asked.

"*Yeah exactly, A Jew from Brooklyn,*" I said.

"Or in my case *A Jew Grows in Brooklyn,*" added Jake.

"That's it!" I said. "That's it!"

"What?"

"That's the name of the show!"

"Let me think about it," said Jake.

"Think about it? Are you crazy? Think about it!? It's perfect! It's a funny title and besides it has the words 'Jew' and 'Brooklyn' in it. Who in New York wouldn't come see it?"

And they did come, and they did see it, and now it's touring the nation. So, when Jake called me up and said he was going to write a book, I never doubted it for a minute.

My direct involvement with the show ended with the New York City run. It was Jake's show (heck, it was Jake's life!), so Jake was perfectly able to guide it and refine it as the months went on. I was at Jake's house after about two years of touring. Jake handed me a check.

"What's this for?"

"Well, I just figured you should get something for each week of the tour."

"But that wasn't in my contract," I said.

No, it wasn't in *my* contract. But it was in Jake's contract. The one he had inside himself. Remember? Gem Upholstery. Remember? "Be like your father. Your father was an honest man. Be like your father."

—Jon Huberth

AN ARTICLE
BY JONAH EHRENREICH

I've said a lot about my dad in this book, and I wanted to let him speak for himself a bit. It was so hard to pick one piece from his hundreds of published articles and writings, but I finally chose the article that follows, which I refer to earlier in the book. On the same day President Ronald Reagan, along with a joint resolution of Congress, declared Kristallnacht remembrance week in the United States, and the first cornerstone was laid for the Holocaust Museum in Washington, my father wrote the following.

"WHY DON'T I ALSO HAVE A GRANDMOTHER?"

Tomorrow it will be 50 years since that infamous day in 1938, when the Nazis staged their Kristallnacht (Night of Broken Glass)—an orgy of hate, violence and murder throughout Germany and Austria. Jewish houses of worship were burned, business places were destroyed and innocent people were beaten, arrested and murdered for the sin of being Jewish. This savagery was perpetuated in the middle of civilized Europe. As unbelievable as it was at that time, we now know that those heinous events were only a pale shadow of what these barbarians of the 20th century had in store for the people of Eastern Europe, and especially for the Jewish people.

President Roosevelt, when he recalled the American ambassador in protest against the events of Kristallnacht, stated, "We can scarcely believe such things occur in our 20th century civilization." Since Kristallnacht was so horrifying, how much more so were the events of the seven long years of the Holocaust. Compared with the horrors of the ghettos, concentration camps and gas chambers that followed, the fires and atrocities of Kristallnacht almost appear tame, as macabre and unbelievable as this may seem.

Even I, the only survivor of a large family, have moments when I find it hard to believe that all those horrors really happened. At such times I recall an event of thirty years ago. My 4-year-old son was playing in the street with other children. One child was called by his grandmother for a hug and a treat. My son came in crying and asked, "Why don't I also have a grandmother?" He doesn't. Nor does he have a grandfather or aunts, uncles and cousins. To me, the Holocaust is not only real, but is still happening to me and my children.

Martin Niemoeller, a German pastor, spent seven years in a concentration camp. He wrote:

"First they came for the Jews and I did not speak out—because I was not a Jew.

"Then they came for the Socialists, and I did not speak out—because I was not a Socialist.

"Then they came for the trade unionists, and I did not speak out—because I was not a trade unionist.

"Then they came for me—and there was no one left to speak out for me."

It was almost too late for the peoples of Europe. There is no doubt what might have happened if the Nazis became the first to develop nuclear arms. Yes, it was almost too late for the peoples of Europe, but for my people, the Jews of Eastern Europe, it was not "almost"—but indeed too late. What else can one say when of the 3.5 million Jews in pre-war Poland, only 5,000 elderly persons are left. A similar situation exists in the other lands of Eastern Europe. True, the Jewish people many times in their long history came back from the brink of disaster and they will do so again. But the East European branch of the Jewish people, the source of Western Judaism, will alas be no more.

While remembering Kristallnacht, we realize that not only Jews were the victims of the barbaric Nazi hordes—the inventors of the most ghastly methods and instruments of human extermination. Many millions of other nationalities of Eastern Europe became innocent victims of the Nazis. Even today the whole world suffers as a direct result of the Kristallnacht and its aftermath, the Holocaust. If today human life has become more dispensable than ever, and state-promoted terrorism and genocide is going on, it is a direct result of the legacy Kristallnacht and the Holocaust.

To be sure, the world was never a place of perfect peace. Bloodshed and wars were part of life since the beginning of time. But wars were waged in the name of perceived goals, whether territorial, economic, or ideological. Once a goal was either achieved or abandoned, the bloodshed stopped. At the time of the Kristallnacht and during the Holocaust, violence and genocide had become the main goal. This is especially true in the case of the Jewish people. This was documented by the fact that towards the end of World War II, when the German army was in retreat, railroad cars that were badly needed by the army were diverted instead to transport the Jewish people to the various death camps for annihilation. So strong was the evil power of hatred.

Sadly, even at this time there are still groups obsessed with hate, but as long as people of good will remember the lessons of Kristallnacht and the Holocaust and are willing to stand guard in the defense of freedom and justice, these groups will not succeed in poisoning the world again with their hatred.

While visiting Vienna, April 19, 1985, Pope John Paul II said, ". . . The fate of the Jewish community, once so fruitfully integrated into the nations of Europe now so tragically decimated, admonishes us to seize every opportunity for promoting human and spiritual understanding, so that we can stand before God together, and to serve humanity in God's spirit."

It is in that spirit that we should observe the anniversary of Kristallnacht, thereby showing our outrage and proclaiming our willingness to be counted on the side of freedom, justice and humanity. So let us remember, light a candle or say a prayer for the innocent victims of that tragic era.

First published in the Times Herald Record *November 8, 1988.*

ABOUT THE AUTHOR

Jake Ehrenreich is an accomplished musician, actor, playwright, singer, and comedian, and spent the last few years starring in his stage show *A Jew Grows in Brooklyn,* which broke box-office records in the heart of Broadway and now plays to sold out audiences and critical acclaim across the nation.

Jake performed on Broadway in *Dancin'*, *Barnum,* and *They're Playing Our Song,* and toured internationally as Ringo in *Beatlemania.* He starred for Joseph Papp at the Public Theater Shakespeare Festival in the title role of *Jonah,* and Off-Broadway performances include *Songs Of Paradise, The Golden Land,* and *A Hot Minute.*

Jake was featured vocalist and emcee at New York's Rainbow Room, sung numerous Radio and TV "jingles," and has headlined at national conventions for major corporations including American Express, Johnson and Johnson, Walt Disney, and many others.

Jake recently recorded a CD dedicated to his father called *Yiddish Unplugged,* a children's CD in fifteen languages called *Songs for Little Planet,* and has begun filming *The Jake Ehrenreich Show,* a variety TV show. A documentary based on his life story is currently in production.

Jake lives with this wife, Lisa, and eleven-year-old son, Dovy, in Upstate New York.